STRANGERS AND PILGRIMS

A Novel

BY THE AUTHOR OF

'LADY AUDLEY'S SECRET'

ETC. ETC. ETC.

' Egypt, thou knewst too well,
My heart was to thy rudder tied by the strings,
And thou shouldst tow me after; o'er my spirit
Thy full supremacy thou knewst; and that
Thy beck might from the bidding of the gods
Command me.'

IN THREE VOLUMES

VOL. III.

LONDON
JOHN MAXWELL AND CO.
4 SHOE LANE, FLEET STREET
1873
[All rights reserved]

This scarce antiquarian book is included in our special *Legacy Reprint Series*. In the interest of creating a more extensive selection of rare historical book reprints, we have chosen to reproduce this title even though it may possibly have occasional imperfections such as missing and blurred pages, missing text, poor pictures, markings, dark backgrounds and other reproduction issues beyond our control. Because this work is culturally important, we have made it available as a part of our commitment to protecting, preserving and promoting the world's literature. Thank you for your understanding.

STRANGERS AND PILGRIMS

Book the Third.

CHAPTER V.

> 'I strive to number o'er what days
>   Remembrance can discover,
> Which all that life or earth displays
>   Would lure me to live over.
> There rose no day, there roll'd no hour
>   Of pleasure unembitter'd;
> And not a trapping deck'd my power
>   That gall'd not while it glitter'd.'

THEY were at Slogh-na-Dyack, in Argyleshire, where, at the foot of a heather-clothed mountain that ran up almost perpendicularly to meet the skies, Lord Paulyn had bought for himself a palatial abode, in that Norman-Gothic style which pervades the mansions of the North—a massive pile of building flanked by sugar-loaf towers, with one tall turret dominating the rest, as a look-out for the lord of the castle when it was his fancy to sweep the waters with his falcon gaze. It is almost impossible to imagine a more delicious habitation, sheltered front and rear by those lofty hills, the blue waters of the Kyles of Bute lapping against its garden terrace; a climate equal to Torquay; long ranges of orchard houses where peaches and nectarines ripened as under Italian skies; orangeries, vineries, pineries; stabling of unlimited capacity, but chiefly devoted to such sturdy ponies as could best tread those rugged mountain roads; verily, all that the soul of a Solomon himself, in the plenitude of his power and riches, could desire; in the golden autumn, when the grain was still ripening for the late northern harvest, making patches of vivid yellow here and there upon the gentler slopes at the base of the opposite hills, when the purple heather, like a Roman Emperor's mantle, was spread over the mountain.

The Norman castle was none of Lord Paulyn's building. Not in those mediæval fancies of keep and donjon, not in those architectural caprices of machicolated battlements and elaborately-carved mullions, did the heir of all the Paulyns squander that wealth which the dowager had accumulated by unheard-of scrapings and pinchings and self-denials during his long minority. The château of Slogh-na-Dyack had been erected at the cost of a millionaire Glasgow manufacturer, who had made his money out of knife-powder and scouring-paper, and who, when he had built for himself this lordly dwelling-house, had the mortification of discovering that neither his wife nor children would consent to abide there. The heather-clad mountain, the blue water, the wide bosom of Loch Fyne stretching away in the distance, the wild denizens of that mountain region, the flutter of whose strong wings gladdened the heart of the sportsman, might be all very well; and to three or four weeks at Rothesay or Colintrave in the bathing season the lady and her daughters had no objection; but a fixed residence, six months out of the twelve, on that lonely shore, they steadfastly refused to endure. So the scouring-paper and knife-powder manufacturer, to whom the cost of a Norman castle more or less was a mere bagatelle, gave his agent orders to dispose of the château at the earliest opportunity, and resigned himself to the sacrifice involved in such a sale. The house and its appurtenances had cost him five-and-twenty thousand, the land five. He sold the whole to Lord Paulyn—after prolonged haggling, in which at last the Glasgow manufacturer showed himself unequal to the English nobleman—for seventeen thousand, and went home, after signing the contract, to his mansion by the West Park, rejoiced to be rid of his useless toy.

Lord Paulyn had been chiefly attracted to the place by its peculiar capacities for the abode of a yachting man. Slogh-na-Dyack stood on the edge of a bay, where there was anchorage for half-a-dozen yachts of the largest calibre; while on one side of the mansion there was a narrow inlet to a secondary harbour, a bay within a bay, a little basin hollowed out of the hills, where, when tempests were raging, the frailest bark might ride secure, so perfect was the shelter, so lofty the natural screen that fenced it from the winds. It was a harbour for fairies, a calm lakelet in which, on moonlit nights, one would have scarcely been surprised to find Titania and her company sporting with the silvern spray.

Hither Reginald Paulyn brought his wife after they had been married about two years and a half. It was her first visit, except for a flying glimpse of those mountain slopes from her husband's yacht, to Scotland—*his* land, her first lover's native land. The thought thrilled her even now, when the remembrance of the days in which he had loved her was like the memory of a dream.

She had been married two years and a half; years in which she had drained the cup of worldly pleasure, and of womanly sorrow also, to the very lees. She had run riot in fashionable extravagances; given some of the most popular parties in London, in the house with the many balconies; won for herself the brilliant distinction that attends social success; queened it over all compeers by the insolence of her beauty, the dash and sparkle of her manner. For a little while—so long as the glamour lasted, and selfishness was subjugated by the intoxication of novelty—she had ruled her husband; then had come disputes, in which she had been for the chief part triumphant; then later disputes, in which his dogged strength of will had conquered; then coldness, severance, estrangement, each tugging at the chain, eager to go his or her own way. But before the world—that world for which Elizabeth had chosen to live—Lord and Lady Paulyn appeared still a very happy young couple, a delightful example of that most delightful fact in natural history—a love match.

Their quarrels at the worst, and they had been exceedingly bitter, had hardly been about the most serious things upon which men and women could disagree. Money matters, my lady's extravagance, had been the chief disturbing influence. The breast of neither husband nor wife had been troubled with the pangs of jealousy. Elizabeth's conduct as a matron was irreproachable. In the very vortex of fashionable frivolity no transient breath of suspicion had ever tarnished the brightness of her name. The Viscount, in his unquestionable liberty, had ample room and verge enough for any sin against his marriage vow were he inclined to be a sinner, but as yet Elizabeth had never stooped to suspect. Their estrangement therefore had not its root in those soul-consuming jealousies which sunder some unions. Their disputes were of a more sordid nature, the wranglings of two worldly-minded beings bent on their own selfish pleasures.

Eighteen months after their marriage there came the one real affliction of Elizabeth's womanhood. A son had been born to her, fair as the first offspring of youth and beauty, a noble soul—or so it seemed to her—looking out of those clear childish eyes, a child who had the inspired seraphic look of the holy Babe in a picture by Raffaelle, and whose budding nature gave promise of a glorious manhood. He was only a few months old—a few months which made up the one pure and perfect episode in Elizabeth's life—when he was taken away from her, not lost without bitterest struggles, vainest fondest hopes, deepest despair. For a little while after his death the mother's life also hung in the balance, reason tottered, darkness and horror shut out the light. Dragged through this tangle of mind and body, no one seeming to know very clearly which was out of joint, by physic which seemed to hinder or nature which finally healed, the bereaved mother went back to the world, and tried to strangle grief in the endless coil of pleasure; worked harder than a horse at a mill, and smiled sometimes with a heart that ached to agony; had brief flashes of excitement that seemed like happiness; defied memory; tried to extinguish regret for the tender being she had loved in a more exclusive devotion to self; grew day by day harder and more worldly; lost even the power to compassionate the distress of others, saying to herself in a rebellious spirit, 'Is there any sorrow like unto my sorrow?'

To Lord Paulyn the loss of his first-born had been a blow, but not an exceeding heavy one. He had considered the baby a fine little fellow, had caressed him, and tossed him in the air occasionally, at somewhat remote intervals, after the approved fashion of fathers, while smirking nurses marvelled at his lordship's condescension; but he was not broken down by the loss of him. He was a young man, and was not in a desperate hurry for an heir. He had something of that feeling which monarchs have been said to entertain upon the subject of their eldest sons, an inclination to regard the heir-apparent as a *memento mori.*

'By Jove, you know, it isn't the liveliest thing to look forward to,' he had said to his friends when arguing upon the subject in the abstract; 'a young fellow who'll go and dip himself up to the hilt with a pack of money-lenders, and borrow on post-obits, and play old gooseberry with his father's estate by the time he is twenty-one, and perhaps make a finish by marrying a ballet-girl before he's twenty-two.'

It was after a season of surpassing brilliancy, an unbroken round of gaieties, involving the expenditure of so much money that Lord Paulyn groaned and gnashed his teeth when the butler brought in the midsummer bills—a season which had ended in the most serious quarrel Elizabeth and her husband had ever had—that the Viscount brought his wife to this Norman château, not in love but in anger, intending this banishment to the coast of Argyle as a means of bringing the lady to a due sense of her iniquities and a meek submission to his will.

'She'll find it rather difficult to get rid of money *there*,' he said to himself, with a sardonic grin, 'and I shall take care to fill the house with visitors of my own choosing. There'll be Hilda, too, to look after *my* interest. Yes, I think I shall have the upper hand at Slogh-na-Dyack.'

This was another change which the last year had brought to pass. Just at the end of the London season—happening so opportunely after the last ball at Buckingham Palace, as Madame Passementerie, the French milliner, ventured to remark to Lady Paulyn's maid, Gimp—the noble house of Paulyn had been thrown into mourning by the demise of the dowager.

'The noble lady had led a life of extreme seclusion throughout a prolonged widowhood,' said the obituary notice in a fashionable journal; 'thus offering the most touching tribute which affection can pay to those it has cherished while on earth, and still fondly mourns when transferred to a higher sphere. Honoured and beloved alike by equals and dependents, she was the centre and source of all good to those who came within her peaceful circle, and she was followed to her last resting-place in the family vault in old Ashcombe church by a train of friends, tenants, and retainers, in which long procession of mourners there was not one who did not lament the loss of a valued friend or an honoured benefactress.' The notice had been written for another patrician widow, but served very well for Lady Paulyn, about whom the editors of newspapers knew little or nothing. She had lived a retired life in the depths of the country, and it was argued that she must of necessity have been benevolent and beloved.

Her death, at the age of seventy-four, had been occasioned by an accident. Sitting up one night in her dressing-room after the household had retired, poring over her agent's last accounts, she had set fire to her cap, an elaborate construction of blonde and ribbons, and had been a good deal burnt about the head and face before Hilda, who slept in an adjacent room, and was promptly awakened by her screams, could rush to her rescue.

Her constitution, vigorous to the last, held out for a little while against grim death, but the shock proved too much for the aged frame, whose sap and muscle had been wasted by the asceticism of economy. The dowager died a few hours after telegrams and express trains had brought her son to her bed-side.

As she had only consented to be just barely civil to Elizabeth in their unfrequent intercourse, it was not to be supposed that her departure from this world could be a profound affliction to the reigning Viscountess. She was sorry that her mother-in-law's death should have been a painful one, and perhaps that was all.

'What a pity old people can't die like that person in Mrs. Thrales' *Three Warnings*!' she said afterwards. 'Death ought to come quietly to fetch them, without any unnecessary suffering; only a natural surprise and annoyance at being taken away against one's will, like a child that is fetched home from a nursery ball.'

The Viscount contemplated his bereavement chiefly from a business-like point of view.

'I am afraid the Devonshire estates will go to pot now my poor mother's gone,' he said dolefully. 'I shall never get any one to screw the tenants as she did. That agent fellow, Lawson, was only a cipher. It was the old woman who really did the work, and kept them up to collar. I shall feel the difference now she's gone, poor old soul!'

'I suppose Miss Disney will go into lodgings at Torquay or somewhere, and live upon her private means,' said Elizabeth, hardly looking up from the pages of a new novel she was skimming, seated luxuriously in one of the Park-lane balconies, in a very bower of summer blossoms, kept in perennial bloom by the minions of the nurseryman.

This sounded as if she had forgotten a certain conversation in a Devonshire lane one dusky March evening.

'I thought I told you that Hilda had no means,' answered the Viscount rather gloomily. 'She must come to live with us, of course.'

'What, in our house, where we live! Won't that be rather like that strange person who lives over somewhere beyond the Rocky Mountains, and has ever so many wives? I'm sure, if Miss Disney is to live with us, I shall feel myself a number two.'

'I wish you wouldn't talk such confounded nonsense, Elizabeth. I suppose you pick up that sort of thing from your friends, who all seem to talk the same jargon, turning up their noses at everybody in creation.'

'No, but seriously, can't Miss Disney go on living at Ashcombe? I should think *she* ought to be able to screw the tenants; she must have learnt your poor mother's ways.'

'Miss Disney will have a home in my house, wherever it is. And I think you ought to be uncommonly glad to get hold of a sensible young woman for a companion. As to my keeping up a separate establishment at Ashcombe for one person's accommodation, that's too preposterous an idea to be entertained for a moment. I shall try and let the place as it stands. You'll be thankful enough for her society, I daresay, at Slogh-na-Dyack.'

'I shall have the hills and the sea,' said Elizabeth; 'they will be better company for me than Miss Disney.'

She had seen the château in the course of a yachting expedition in the autumn of last year, when the Viscount, sorely alarmed by the nature of the illness that had followed the loss of her boy, had taken her to roam the blue waters in quest of health and spirits. Health and spirits had come, in some measure—health that was fitful, spirits that were apt to be forced and spurious, a laugh that had a false ring in it, mirth which sounded sweet enough at one time, but jangled, out of tune, and harsh at another.

So the Viscount wrote to inform Hilda Disney that henceforth her life was to be spent in his household—wrote as briefly and unceremoniously as he might have written to a housemaid—and a week later Miss Disney came to Park-lane, covered with crape, pale, placid, impenetrable. Elizabeth made a great effort over herself in order to receive this new-comer with some faint show of kindness.

'I hope you two mean to get on well together,' said the Viscount, in a little speech that sounded like a command.

'I have no doubt we shall get on remarkably well —if we don't interfere with each other,' answered

Elizabeth. 'I believe that is the secret of a harmonious household.'

This was an intimation designed to give Miss Disney a correct idea of her position, a hint which that young lady fully comprehended.

She accepted this position with a certain quiet grace which might have won the heart of any one who had a heart to be won. Elizabeth's had been given away twice over, once to Malcolm Forde, once to her lost baby. Her small stock of love had been spent on these two. There was no room in her cold weary heart for anything but the ashes of that old fire—certainly no admission for Hilda Disney. But as at this stage of affairs that young person appeared content to be a cipher in her new home, Elizabeth's languid indifference was not kindled into active dislike. She tolerated the intruder, but at the same time avoided her. This was the position of affairs when Lord Paulyn and a few chosen friends began life and grouse-shooting on the moors around Slogh-na-Dyack.

To Elizabeth's jaded spirits, worn out by the small excitements of society, the change was at first a welcome one. It was pleasant to find herself mistress of a new domain, which differed widely from her other dominions. Very pleasant to be remote from the region of racehorses and trainers, and trial gallops and experimental exercise of rival two-year olds, in the dewy dawn of autumnal mornings; trials in which, out of mere politeness, she had been obliged sometimes to affect an interest. The novelty of the Norman castle and its surroundings delighted her; nor was she discouraged by its seclusion, or particularly afflicted by the usurpation of the limited number of spare bedrooms by her husband's sporting cronies, whereby she was deprived of the society of half-a-dozen or so of her own dearest friends, whose reception she had planned as one of the amusements of her Scottish home. The architect whose mediæval mind had designed Slogh-na-Dyack had refused to fritter away his space upon spare bedrooms, reserving his resources for sugar-loaf turrets, donjons, keeps, Gothic balconies, perforated battlements, picture-galleries, a banqueting-hall with a groined roof and a musicians' gallery, a tennis-court, and a cloistered walk under the drawing-room floor.

'You will have to build me a new wing next year, Reginald,' Lady Paulyn observed, after expressing her general approval of the château. 'It is all very well for us to exist in this benighted manner—for I don't count your shooting people as visitors—for once in a way, but we couldn't possibly exist here another year without a dozen or so more rooms.'

'Couldn't we?' said the Viscount, putting on his sullen air, which meant war to the knife. 'I chose Slogh-na-Dyack just because it was a little out of the beaten track—not much though, for people go to Oban nowadays just as they used to go to Brighton—and because it has precious little accommodation for your cackling brood of dear friends, no stowage for French waiting-maids and such rubbish—a place where I could feel myself master, and where I might expect you would even take the trouble to devote a little time to my society.'

Elizabeth yawned.

'To hear you talk about shooting innocent birds, and of what your horses are going to do next year, and what they ought to have done, but did not do, this year. What a pity there should be such a sameness in domestic conversation!'

'I suppose you would like it better if I could talk about converting the heathen,' snarled the Viscount. It was not the first time he had tried to sting his wife with an allusion to the lover who jilted her.

'I should like it better if you had a mind wide enough to be interested in human beings, instead of in dogs and horses,' she answered, flashing out at him passionately.

Miss Disney was a mute witness of this little scene, but a mere cipher, whose presence had no restraining influence.

'I shall not think of coming here next year unless there are some more rooms built,' Elizabeth remarked decisively, after a little more skirmishing.

'We needn't talk about coming next year until we have quite made up our minds to go away. This place has a famous winter climate,' said the Viscount, looking into a huge sealskin case, as if in search of some rare species of cigar, the selection whereof was a work of time. He had a knack of looking down when he said disagreeable things.

'I could not endure the place for more than two months,' replied his wife, 'and I have made engagements for December.'

'That's a pity; for I have invited some fellows here for Christmas.'

'I am sure you are at liberty to entertain them—with Miss Disney's assistance. I shall resign all my privileges as châtelaine at the end of November.'

'We'll see about that,' said Lord Paulyn darkly. But as he had often uttered this mystic threat, and nothing had ever come of it, except that Elizabeth had always had her own way in spite of him, the lady was not appalled by his dark speech.

It is not to be supposed that Lady Paulyn was always uncivil to her husband, that she flouted him in season and out of season. She had her intervals of sunshine and sweetness; smiled upon him as she did upon society, and with almost as empty a smile; bewitched him even with something of the old witchery; for, despite his numerous aggravations, he still admired her, and still fondly believed her the handsomest woman in Europe.

This was the state of affairs when Hilda Disney first entered their household; but their domestic life underwent a gradual change after her coming. It was as if by some subtle influence she widened the gulf between them, without design, without malice, but only by her presence. If she had been a statue, she could scarcely have seemed more innocent of evil intention, more unconscious of the harm she did; yet she parted them irrevocably.

She offended the wife by no demonstrative affection for the husband; yet, by an unobtrusive concern for his comfort, a perpetual solicitude, an unsleeping care of his well-being, shown in the veriest trifles, but shown almost hourly, she made his wife's indifference a thousand times more obvious than it had ever been before. By her interest in his conversation, by her appreciation of his vapid jokes, her acute perception of the smallest matters in which his prosperity or success was involved, she reminded him of his wife's utter apathy about all these things. One of the grievances of his married life was the fact that he had never been able to interest Elizabeth in the details of his racing stud, those narrow chances and hairbreadth failures which make or mar the fortunes of the year. She liked Epsom and Ascot and Newmarket and Goodwood and Doncaster and York well enough as scenes of gaiety and excitement—festivals in which her beauty made her a kind of queen. She could even admire a winning horse as a grand and famous creature; but she had not a mathematical brain, and could not by any means comprehend that intricate process of calculation by which great results are sometimes arrived at in the racing world, and by which the Napoleons of the turf accumulate their colossal fortunes.

In this she was the very reverse of Hilda, whose arithmetical powers had been trained to extreme acuteness in the service of the late dowager, and who, without any natural fondness for horses, could enter into all the complications of a betting-book; could even, on some rare occasion, give a wrinkle to the

Viscount himself, as that gentleman remarked with supreme astonishment.

'Upon my word, you know, Hilda, you're the downiest bird—I beg your pardon, the cleverest woman I ever met with. If my wife had only your brains—'

'With her own beauty! That would be too much. Not that my brains are anything to boast of, but I have been trained in a rather severe school.'

'I should think you have indeed; my mother was an out-and-outer. I don't believe there ever was such a screw, you know, before her time, or ever will be after it. There ought to be something of the kind put up in Ashcombe church, by Jove. It would look well in Latin—that quotation of Burke's, for instance: *Magnum vectigal est parsimonia.* But you have got a wider way of looking at this than my mother. And as for looks, if you're not as handsome as Elizabeth, who really is the finest woman in Europe, you've no reason to complain of your share of good looks; and you know there was a day when I used to say a good deal more than that.'

A faint colour came into Hilda's fair face.

'We were children then,' she said.

'O, hang it; I was at Oxford, and in the University eight. There wasn't much of the child about me, Hilda.'

'Except in a childish want of judgment—not knowing your own mind, in short,' she answered, looking down at a flimsy printed catalogue of race-horses which they had been studying together when this conversation began.

'O, well, we settled all that ever so long ago. Let bygones be bygones, Hilda.'

'Was it I who recalled the past?'

'I'm sure it wasn't I,' answered Lord Paulyn hastily, 'and I don't want to recall it. I don't forget what a temper you had in those days, Hilda. Children indeed! You were a child who knew how to call a fellow over the coals like anything. I've a very keen recollection of some of our shindies. However, all that was so long ago, and I'm an old married man now; so I thought we should be able to get on very well together. And I must say you're wonderfully improved; ten years' more grinding in my mother's mill has made a difference, hasn't it?'

'I hope I have conquered my evil tempers, and everything else that was foolish in me,' said Hilda meekly.

That little demure speech of Miss Disney's set the Viscount thinking. Ten years ago there had been certain love-passages between himself and his cousin—a pretty little pastoral flirtation, which filled the intervals of his field sports pleasantly enough—but which, begun for the amusement of long dull autumnal afternoons in a dreary old house, ended somewhat seriously. The girl had been serious from the beginning. Her cousin, Reginald, was the only man whose society had ever brightened the dismalities of her joyless home. He was young, good-looking, energetic, and possessed that superfluity of physical strength which gives a kind of dash and swagger to a man's manner of doing things—a dash and swagger that, in the eyes of inexperienced girlhood, pass for courage and chivalry. He rode well, shot superbly, talked the last Oxonian slang, the novelty of which language was agreeable after the dowager's dull grumblings and perpetual prosing upon small worries. In a word, he was the only thing Hilda Disney had to love, and she loved him, hiding more intensity than he could have suspected under her placid demeanour.

For a short time—a long vacation and a Christmas visit—he reciprocated her passion. The fair still face seemed to him the perfection of patrician beauty—a wonderful relief after certain sirens of the barmaid order with whose lighter converse he was wont to soften the asperities of classic learning. He had vague thoughts of a future in which Hilda should be his wife; and was severely rated by his widowed parent upon the folly of his course. Marry Hilda, indeed, without a sixpence, or a rag to her back that was not supplied by charity. He had better pick up a beggar girl in the street at once, and then his next-of-kin would, at least, have the satisfaction of taking out a statute of lunacy on his behalf.

But the passion passed—as passions were apt to pass with the Viscount. A barmaid flirtation—more in earnest than previous barmaid flirtations—blotted out the milder charms of his cousin. When he came to Ashcombe in the next long vacation, he thought her looking pale and faded. Nor was her temper improved. She perceived his indifference, and taxed him with it. Then came bitter little speeches, sudden bursts of tears, angry rushes from the room, bangings of doors, and all the varieties of squabbling that compose lovers' quarrels; until at last, with a praiseworthy candour, the Viscount confessed that he had for some time past ceased to care for his cousin, except in the most cousinly way.

'If ever you're in want of a friend, you know, Hilda, you can come to me; and wherever I live—by and by, when my mother goes off the hooks—my house will be your home, if you haven't one of your own.'

She acknowledged this offer with some dignity, but with a very white face and lips that quivered faintly in spite of her firmness, and expressed the hope that she might never intrude upon his hospitality.

'Well, I hope you'll make a good match, Hilda,' he said, rather awkwardly, 'and then, of course, you'll be independent of me and mine; but I shall never forget you, and how fond I was of you, and all that. O, by the way, you may as well give me back the letters I wrote you from Oxford. One never knows when that sort of rubbish may fall into dangerous hands, and make no end of mischief. Hunt 'em all up, will you, Hilda? and we'll amuse ourselves with a bonfire this wet morning.'

Hilda informed him, after a few moments' hesitation, that she had made the bonfire already.

'I burnt them one by one as they came, after I had read them once or twice,' she said. 'It was safer on account of my aunt. The surest way of preventing them from falling into dangerous hands.'

'What a deep card you are!—as deep as Garrick, upon my word. You're quite sure you burnt them?'

'Quite sure. Don't be alarmed, Reginald. There will be no action for breach of promise.'

'O, it isn't that, you know. No girl with a

hap'orth of self-respect would go in for that sort of thing; much less such a girl as you. Only old letters are the deuce and all for creating trouble in a man's life. I'm glad you burnt 'em.'

Never since these juvenile love-passages, which left a somewhat unpleasant flavour in Lord Paulyn's mouth—a flavour of remorse, perhaps—had he liked Hilda so well as he liked her now, in their quiet life at Slogh-na-Dyack. She was of so much use to him —so able a counsellor, so ready a confidante. He gave her a pile of his house-steward's bills to look over, and she charmed him at once by suggesting that he should, in future, pay ready money for all household supplies—or make weekly payments, to be ranked as ready money—and claim a discount of ten per cent on all such accounts.

'No doubt the tradesmen pay your people five per cent already,' she said. 'They would willingly pay you ten for the sake of getting ready money. Your discounts ought to pay the wages of half your household, instead of going into the servants' pockets.'

By such brilliant flashes of genius did Hilda charm her cousin. He groaned aloud as he compared this skilled economist with his wife, whose extravagances still rankled in his mind, and whose refusal of a settled allowance he had not ceased to consider an artful stroke of business, whereby she had reserved to herself the right of unlimited expenditure.

'If ever I let her leave Slogh-na-Dyack, I shall restrict her to an allowance of five hundred a year,' he said to himself. But there were times when the spirit of anger against his wife burnt so fiercely within him, that he had serious thoughts of making her spend the rest of her life in Argyleshire, with only such change of scene as his yacht might afford her—a cruise in the Mediterranean now and then, or a run to Madeira or St. Michael's.

'It'll suit me well enough for six months of the year. I can always run up from Glasgow when there are any races on,' reflected Lord Paulyn, who, after the manner of racing men, thought nothing of spending his night in railway carriages, speeding at express rate over the face of the country.

Elizabeth perceived the harmony that reigned between her husband and his cousin; perceived that he no longer troubled himself with the futile endeavour to impart his perplexities to her non-mathematical brain. She saw all this, and without being absolutely jealous—was jealousy possible where love was absent? —was keenly stung by this preference. She had been accustomed to think of her husband as her slave

—a refractory slave sometimes—but never able to put off his bondage; a creature to be made glad by her smile; to be subdued into submission by her frown. She had felt the sense of her power over him all the more keenly because in the society of other women he was, for the most part, morose or indifferent—wrapped up in his own thoughts about his own amusements or speculations—slow to comply with the exigences of polite life; a man who, if he had not been the rich Lord Paulyn, might have been called a boor. To her own chosen friends he had been habitually uncivil—beauty, except her own, seemed to have no charm for him; wit and vivacity only bored him. All the graces of feminine costume were a dead letter.

'I think she wore cherry colour, with blue sleeves,' he answered once, when his wife questioned him upon a fashionable toilette; 'or was it Lord Zetland's colours, white and red? Upon my soul I don't know which.'

She beheld him now for the first time interested in the society of another woman, and beheld with wonder that woman's capacity for understanding him and sympathising with him. Mortified by this discovery, she avenged herself at first by reducing the Viscount's sporting friends to a state of abject slavery; but speedily wearying of this shallow amusement, grew sullen, shut herself up in her own rooms—the best in the house, occupying the whole front of the second story, and sweeping the waters of the strait and the purple hills on the opposite side—read, sketched, and brooded; or roamed alone upon the mountain-side, and thought of her dead-and-gone youth, and the lover she had loved and lost. His image haunted her in this lonely region—in this tranquil, empty life—more than it had ever haunted her since she knelt down upon her bridal eve and prayed to God for strength to forget him. She was in his native country for the first time in her life, and that she should think of him seemed only a natural association of ideas. Nor was this all: she felt herself injured by her husband's evident liking for his cousin's society, and so opened the doors of her heart to fatal memories; lived again as in a dream, her brief summertide of joy and sorrow; gave up her thoughts to sad musings upon that foolish past. Sometimes she varied the burden of that sorrow by thinking of her dead baby—alas! how often in her dreams had she felt those little arms clasped about her neck, those sweet soft breathings on her cheek, and red lips like opening flowers pressed warm against her own! She thought of what that romantic home might have been to her, still blessed with her boy; fancied the sunny noontide on the grassy slope above the blue water, or the terrace sheltered from northern winds by a grove of pinasters; or in the flower-garden behind the house, a fertile hollow at the foot of the mountain; wandering on the mountain top with her darling in her arms, the summer air noisy with loud humming of bees, and the sweet west wind blowing round them. Not for her these tender pleasures, only loneliness and regret; the bitter memory of things that had once been sweet.

Pride stifled all expression of anger at her husband's defection. Not by word or look did she betray her displeasure at the position which Hilda Disney was fast assuming in the household. On the contrary, she suffered the reins to slip from her hands as if weary of the burden of government. Her old languor and dislike to exertion, except in pursuit of some novel pleasure, returned to her. Life at Slogh-na-Dyack was very much like life at Hawleigh Vicarage; there was only a difference of detail. Trained serving-men in place of a parlour-maid; a certain state and splendour in all the machinery of the household. The evenings in the long drawing-room, with its mediæval oak furniture, modern French tapestries, and Brummagem armoury, all made on purpose for the château at the cost of the Glasgow knife-powder maker, were just as dull as the evenings in the old days, when she had yawned over a novel in the society of her three sisters. Lord Paulyn and his guests congregated in the smoking-room, or paced the wide stone hall, a spacious vaulted chamber always odorous with tobacco, or strolled on the terrace, staring at the moonlit water, and talking of their day's work among the birds. They were men who walked thirty miles or so between breakfast and dinner, and who, after devoting a couple of hours to their evening gorge, retired within themselves like boa-constrictors, and were in no manner dependent upon feminine society. So when Elizabeth, weary of their vapid compliments, and despising the petty triumph afforded by the subjugation of such small deer, ceased to be particularly civil to them, they deserted the drawing-room almost entirely, and solaced themselves with smoke and billiards, or placid slumbers, stretched at ease upon morocco-covered divans, lulled by the ripple of the wavelets that lapped against the beach.

Once in ten days or so Lord Paulyn sped southward for a day's racing, generally accompanied by a chosen friend, and returned, depressed or elated as the case might be, to talk over all his proceedings—his triumphs or his failures—with his cousin Hilda. These confabulations, which took place openly enough in some snug corner of the drawing-room, wounded Elizabeth to the quick. She began to think that all those vapid men saw the slight thus put upon her, and discussed it in their smoking-room conclaves. She began to fancy that her very servants were losing some touch of their old reverence; that her maid had a compassionate air.

'Shall I live to be pitied?' she asked herself, remembering that she had sold herself to the bondage of a loveless marriage for the sake of being envied.

One day she determined upon sending for Blanche, in order to bring some new force to bear upon Miss Disney; but upon the next day altered her mind. She would not endure that her sister—even her best-loved, most-trusted sister—should see that there was an influence in her husband's house stronger than her own.

'Blanche would go on so,' she said to herself, 'and I feel too weak and tired to bear fuss of any kind. And after all what does it matter if my husband has found somebody to be interested in his racing talk? It never interested me; only I believe that Hilda's sympathy is all put on. No woman could be interested in handicapping and Chester Cups for ever and ever.'

So Lady Paulyn made no struggle to maintain

her authority. She allowed Hilda to drive her pony-carriage, and make friends with the few families scattered in pretty white villas here and there upon the coast. She left to Hilda the trouble of dispensing tea and coffee at the eight-o'clock breakfast; the gentlemen were early at Slogh-na-Dyack, and over the hills and far away before ten. She suffered Hilda to receive the sportsmen when they came straggling up from the boat, with the dogs at their heels, and she rarely appeared herself in the public rooms of the château till a quarter of an hour before the eight-o'clock dinner. She had the long days to herself, and roamed alone where she would, making her companions of the hills and the blue sea. Sometimes, when she looked from the hill-tops towards the Mull of Cantyre, her soul yearned to escape by that rock-bound point, to sail away to the South-Sea isles, and toil, for God's sake, by the side of the man she loved. O, how easy, how sweet, how smooth it seemed to her now, that better life which she had cast away! 'How easy it would have been for me to do good for his sake,' she said; 'to be schooled by him, to become anything that he could make me—a saint almost—by his pure influence!'

Then from that distant seaward opening, from that dream-like gaze towards an unknown world far away, her tired eyes would sink downward to the towers and pinnacles of Slogh-na-Dyack, like a fairy palace dimly seen through the misty atmosphere. Was it not verily the fairy palace of her dreams, symbol of the Cinderella's triumph she had fancied for herself in her childish visions?

'I wonder whether Cinderella was happy,' she said to herself, 'or if she ever wished herself back among the cinders, and hated her fairy godmother for having made her a princess. She found rich husbands for her sisters at any rate, and that is more than I have done. I have been *no* use in the world to any one but myself.'

On quiet Sundays, and the Sabbath at Slogh-na-Dyack was very quiet, the sound of the bells ringing through the soft summer air brought back the thought of Hawleigh and the grave old church, its massive clustered columns and lofty arches, shadowy aisles sonorous with the fresh young voices of the choir, and sometimes with *his* voice alone, reading the lessons of the day, with a tender earnestness that gave familiar words a new meaning. Here in the little Episcopalian chapel the sacred rites were sorely stinted; no white-robed choristers trooping in through the vestry door, no decorated altar-cloths or floral festivals, but the same dull round from year's end to year's end; a harmonium grumbling an accompaniment of common chords to the dullest selection of hymns extant, and one elderly incumbent prosing his feeble little sermons, and doing his best to maintain the dignity of his Church single-handed.

Elizabeth and Miss Disney were regular in their attendance at this small temple, which was an unpretentious edifice of corrugated iron, like a gigantic Dutch oven, until at last, after about half-a-dozen Sundays, Lady Paulyn wearied of the elderly incumbent.

'There's another Episcopalian chapel at Dunallen,' she said; 'a real stone pretty little Gothic building, which can hardly be so intolerably hot as this oven. I shall take the pony-carriage this afternoon, and go over there.'

She did not invite Miss Disney to join her in this expedition; so that young lady, who made a point of holding herself aloof from all intercourse to which she was not specially invited, and who had certainly received no inducement to abandon this reserve, went her own ways to the little iron church in the island, while Lady Paulyn drove to Dunallen. It was a calm sunless afternoon, with an atmosphere that seems made on purpose for Sundays—a day on which the birds forget to sing, and the rabbits lie asleep in their holes. The Kyles of Bute looked smooth as an Italian lake, but there was no Italian sky above them, only the uniform gray of Scottish heavens, unbroken save by the white mist-wreaths on the hill-tops.

The Viscount and his friends, after having spent all the lawful days of the week in perambulating the moors, lunching on the mountain-top upon savoury stews cooked in a travelling kitchener, washed down with Glenlivat, were not sorry for the day of rest, which they devoted to lying full-length on the divans in the smoking-room, or sauntering in the garden and hot-houses, talking Newmarket and Tattersall's. Going to church was not among their accomplishments.

Dunallen was a hamlet among the hills, round which sundry white-stone villas had scattered themselves, a hamlet on a winding hill-side road looking downward across an undulating tract of fertile meadow and cornfield to the blue bosom of the Loch. Lady Paulyn had marked the spot, and the little Gothic Episcopalian church, lately erected at the cost of a land-owner in the neighbourhood, in the course of her lonely rambles. The village was within three miles of Slogh-na-Dyack, and one of her favourite walks was in the moorland above it.

The bells were ringing with a sweet solemn sound in the still air, as the little carriage drove round the curve of the hill, and up to the pretty Gothic doorway of Dunallen chapel. The Presbyterian church stood a few paces off, a gaunt edifice of fifty years ago, grim and uncompromising; as who should say, Here you will get only plain substantial fare, and no foreign kickshaws; something to bite at, in the way of theology. Behind the Episcopalian chapel, with its dainty, dandified air, there rose a little grove of firs upon the green slope of the hill, crowning the Gothic pinnacles with their dark verdure, and in front of the fir-grove, a few yards from the chapel, stood a tiny manse, a miniature Tudor villa, in which a young newly-wedded incumbent might have found life very picturesque and pleasant, but in which there would have hardly been breathing room for a pastor with a large family.

Lady Paulyn was one of the first to enter the small church, and was speedily conducted to a comfortable seat by an obsequious pew-opener, who had marked the arrival of the carriage. The light within was softened by painted windows from Munich; the opened seats were of dark oak; the small temple had the look of a labour of love.

The service was conducted in the usual unornamental style; a little stout man with sandy whiskers read prayers at a hand gallop to a sparse congregation, who afterwards joined their vinegar voices in a shrill hymn, not one of those Hymns Ancient and Modern which Elizabeth loved so well, but a dryas-dust composition, which would never have given wings to any heavenward-soaring soul. Elizabeth thought these ministrations but a small improvement on the services of the corrugated iron chapel at Slogh-na-Dyack. She had fallen into a drowsy absent-minded condition by the time the shrill singing was finished, and did not take the trouble to look up to see the little stout man trot up the pulpit-stairs.

She sat looking down at the loosely-clasped hands in her lap, when another voice, without any preliminary prayer, gave out the text; and lifting her eyes with a wild stare, in which rapture and surprise were strangely blended, saw a tall figure in a surplice in the place where the little man might have stood, the figure of Malcolm Forde.

No cry broke from her lips, though her heart beat as it had never beaten before. She sat dumbly looking at him, white as death, with fixed dilated eyes. The dead newly risen from the grave could not have moved her more deeply. Great Heaven, how she loved him! It seemed to her as if in that moment only she realised the overwhelming force of her love. A new world, a new life, were contained in his presence. To see him there, only to see and hear him—whatsoever gulf yawned between them— was new life to her: renovated youth, hope, joy, enthusiasm, aspiration for higher things.

'O God, if I can only hear his voice every Sunday,' she thought, 'I will worship him, and live for him, and be good and pure for his sake, and never strive to lessen the distance that divides us. What more joy can I desire than to know that he lives, and is well and happy, and breathes the same air I breathe, and looks out across the same sea, and is near me unawares. O, thank God for the chance that brought me to Slogh-na-Dyack! Thank God for my bonnie Scottish home!'

His sermon to-day was like his old sermons, full of life and fire and quiet force and supreme tenderness, the sermon of a man speaking to a cherished flock out of a heart overflowing with love. Yet she fancied that his tones had lost something in mere physical power; that deep-toned voice was weaker than of old. Once he stopped, exhausted, at the close of a sentence, with an appearance of fatigue that she had never seen in him at Hawleigh, and his face looked very pale in the cold light from a northern window.

The thought of this change touched her heart with a sudden sense of fear. That spiritual countenance turned to the northern light, those deep hollow eyes, all the lines of the face more sharply chiselled than of old, something that was not age, but rather an indication of hard wear and tear that stood in the place of age—these were the tokens of his late labours, the seal that his mission had set upon him.

'If he should die,' she said to herself, appalled; 'while I, who seem made of some hard common clay, too tough to be broken by sorrow, go on living.'

The sermon was not a long one. There was no hymn afterwards, only the clink-clink of shillings and sixpences into the bowl, which a grim-looking Scotchman carried round the little church. The service altogether had been of the briefest; and Donald the groom, who perhaps took his measure from a familiarity with the Presbyterian office, had not arrived with the pony-carriage when Lady Paulyn came out of the church.

She looked round her with something like terror at finding herself standing almost alone by the church-door, knowing that Malcolm Forde was so near; might come through that open door at any moment, and meet her face to face, for the first time since he had cast her from his heart with cruel deliberate repudiation.

She thought of the morning on which she had gone to his lodgings in quest of him; gone with a determination to humble herself, to ask for his forgiveness and his blessing before he left her for ever. And behold, that bitter parting, that loss of something which had seemed to her the very life of her life, had not been for ever. The world which seemed so wide was narrow enough to bring these two face to face again.

'If I had seen him that morning, and he had forgiven me, I should never have married Lord Paulyn,' she said to herself. 'If he had left me only a few words of kindness or forgiveness, I would have been true to his memory all my life; but his coldness drove me mad. I had no memory of the past to console me; I had no hope in the future to sustain me.'

Still no sign of Donald and the ponies. The scanty congregation had dispersed; the mountain road was empty. She stood watching the curve round which the ponies must in due time appear, half dreading, half hoping that Malcolm Forde might come that way.

She had been waiting about ten minutes or a

quarter of an hour—a period which seemed almost interminable—when she heard the shutting of a distant door, and the sound of footsteps approaching her. She had gone a little way along the road, in the opposite direction to the vicarage. The incumbent and his friend would be likely to return thither when the service was ended. She had not flung herself purposely in the path of her old lover.

She heard the footsteps drawing nearer, and the voices of two men conversing. One, the thin reedy pipe of the incumbent; the other, that deep graver organ, whose every tone she knew so well.

They had gone a little way past her, when the short stout gentleman, who had been apprised by the appearance of a stray sovereign in the alms-basin that some important member of his flock, or perchance some illustrious stranger, had been among the congregation, turned himself about to behold her, pirouetting in an airy manner, as if admiring the beauties of the landscape.

'Lady Paulyn, I declare,' he murmured to his companion, after a brief survey.

His companion stared at him for a moment with a look of sheer amazement, and stopped short.

' What Lady Paulyn? Do you mean an old woman, Lord Paulyn's mother?'

'No, a young woman, and a very handsome one. The Dowager Lady Paulyn died a few months ago.'

They were walking on again. Malcolm Forde had not looked backward. Was it verily Elizabeth, the woman he had loved, the woman whose image had followed him in his farthest wanderings, the shadowy face looking into his, the spirit voice speaking with him, in spite of his prayer for forgetfulness, in spite of his manhood and his reason? In dreams, walking and sleeping, she had been with him. Thoughts of her had intruded themselves upon his most solemn meditations; never, even at his best, had he been free from those olden fetters, the fatal bondage of earthly love.

And yet he had passed her unawares, upon that mountain road, and would not for all the world go back to speak to her. A few yards farther on they met the pony-carriage, the small cream-coloured ponies with bells upon their harness, the little shell-shaped carriage with its bearskin and scarlet rug.

Mr. Forde smiled his bitterest smile at the sight of that dainty equipage. Was it not for pomps and vanities such as these she had sold herself?

'How does she happen to be here?' he asked his companion.

'You know her!' exclaimed Mr. Mackenzie, the incumbent, turning upon him sharply.

'Yes, I know her.'

'But won't you speak to her? Let us go back. It must seem so rude to have passed her like that. And you can introduce me. I should really have liked to call on her when she first came to Slogh-na-Dyack, but she would naturally attend the Episcopalian church down there, I thought, and I hate the idea of seeming intrusive. Let us go back and speak to her before she drives off.'

'No, Mackenzie. My acquaintance with her began and ended a long time ago. I will not renew it. You must get some one else to present you, or call upon her and present yourself.'

'Was she Lady Paulyn when you knew her?'

'No.'

'Quite a nobody, I've been told, before her marriage?' inquisitively.

'I don't know your exact definition of a nobody. Her father was my vicar—a man of old family; and she was one of the loveliest girls, or I will say the loveliest, I ever saw.'

'No doubt—no doubt; she's a splendid woman now. But it was a great match for a country clergyman's daughter. I wish my daughters may marry half as well when they grow up. Their complexions at present have a tendency to run to freckles; but I daresay they'll grow out of that.'

The pony-carriage flashed rapidly by at this moment; Elizabeth driving, and looking neither to the right nor left.

'How do they come to be here?' asked Malcolm.

'What, didn't I tell you yesterday, when I took you for that long round? No, by the bye, we did not go near Slogh-na-Dyack. Lord Paulyn has lately bought a place on the coast here; a charming place, which he got a dead bargain. We'll go over and call to-morrow, if you like.'

'Haven't I told you that I don't want to renew my acquaintance with Lady Paulyn?'

'That sounds so ungracious; your old vicar's daughter too. However, I suppose you have your own reasons.'

'I have. It's best to tell you the plain truth, perhaps; only mind it goes no farther, not even to Mrs. Mackenzie. Miss Luttrell and I were engaged to be married, and she flung me over for Lord Paulyn. That's the whole story. It's a thing of the remote past; a folly on both sides, no doubt; since she was created by nature to adorn the position she now occupies, and I had other hopes which I was willing to abandon for her sake. Do not think that I cherish any ill-feeling against her; only—only it might pain us both to meet.'

Mr. Mackenzie held his peace after this, and the two men made a circuit of the hill-side, and returned to the manse to dine on a cold roast of beef, as Mrs. Mackenzie called it, and a salad, in clerical fashion; content to consume their viands cold on the day of rest. But Mr. Mackenzie had a budget of news for his wife that night when they retired to their own chamber, and dutifully poured into her listening ear the story of Malcolm Forde's love-affair.

CHAPTER VI.

'Quel mortel ne sait pas, dans le sein des orages,
Où reposer sa tête, à l'abri des naufrages?
Et moi, jouet des flots, seul avec mes douleurs,
Aucun navire ami ne vient frapper ma vue,
Aucun, sur cette mer où ma barque est perdue,
Ne porte mes couleurs.'

THREE months before the Sunday on which Elizabeth went to the little Episcopal church among the hills, Malcolm Forde had come home, a very shadow of his former self, to renew the strength that he had spent in the fatiguing service of his mission. Not disheartened or disgusted with his work did he journey homeward, only intent upon returning to that beloved labour in a little while, with a frame made vigorous by the cool breezes of his native land, and mental powers that should have gained new force from a brief season of rest. Infinitely had God blest his endeavours in that distant world, and infinite were his hopes of future achievement. He had not mistaken his mission upon this earth; the work prospered under his hand. He was of that stamp of men who are by nature formed to be leaders of their fellow-men; created to convince, to subjugate, to rule the weaker clay which makes the mass of humanity.

He came home to Scotland in no manner depressed, though he felt that his health was shaken; that he had laboured just a little longer than prudential considerations would have warranted; not cast down, although he fancied sometimes, as the good ship sailed homewards, that he should never again cross those blue waters, never finish the work so well begun.

'If not I, some other one,' he said to himself, in tranquil resignation. 'I cannot believe that labourers will be wanted for so fair a vineyard. Let me be content if I have been suffered to see the beginning of that glorious end which I know must come in God's good time, before that wonderful day when the dead shall arise from their graves, and Alice Fraser and I shall see each other again.'

He thought of his first love, whose bridal robe had been her winding-sheet, whose undefiled image rose before him, pure and stainless as an angel's; and then, with unspeakable bitterness, he thought of that other love, so much more fatally beloved, who had stained her soul with the deep shame of a loveless marriage; who had bartered purity and truth and honour, her life's liberty, her soul's independence, for the pomps and vanities of this world.

He went back to Lenorgie. Those he had best loved were sleeping their quiet sleep in the old churchyard among the hills; but there were old friends still left to give him cordial welcome, and he spent the drowsy summer time pleasantly enough in the restful calm of his native place. His small estate was let to strangers, even the house in which he was born; but he found a comfortable lodging in one of the farmhouses on his own land. He had just sufficient society to make life agreeable, and ample leisure for making himself acquainted with the better part of that mass of literature which had been produced during his absence; literature whereof very little had reached him on the other side of the Pacific.

In this manner he spent a couple of months; then, finding his health in some manner restored, started on a walking tour from Loch Rannoch to Loch Lomond, resting wherever the fancy seized him; sometimes spending half a week at some quiet out-of-the-way inn, where the herd of summer tourists came not; fishing a little, reading and thinking a great deal, with hope that grew stronger as his physical strength revived; taking the business of pedestrianism altogether quietly, and varying his work according to the humour of the hour. Thus, after the best part of a month spent upon ground which the British tourist scours in a couple of days, he came to Dunallen, where he had an old High-School and college comrade of days gone by, in the person of the Rev. Peter Mackenzie, whose duty he had promised to take upon his own hands for a couple of months, while Mr. Mackenzie and his family enjoyed a holiday in Belgium.

For the first week of Mr. Forde's residence the Rev. Peter was to remain at Dunallen, in order to introduce his friend to his new duties, and make him feel at home in the snug little Gothic manse on the hill-side, which was a great deal too small for the Mackenzie olive-branches, but was so arranged, with infinite management on the part of Mrs. Mackenzie, as to contain a permanent spare bedroom. The juvenile Mackenzies inhabited certain dovecot-like chambers in the gables, which might have been rather large for a pigeon, but were a good deal too small for a child, except upon the principle that nature will adapt itself to anything in the way of surroundings. The little Mackenzies might have carried their bedrooms on their back like snails without being very heavily burdened; but they thrived and flourished notwithstanding, and whooped and gambolled like young scions of the Macgregor family in that clear mountain air. In this hospitable abode, where he was almost killed, as Juliet proposed to slay Romeo, with much cherishing, Mr. Forde intended to repose himself for seven or eight weeks, counting the light duties of this small parish as the next thing to idleness, before returning to his labours at the other end of the world. He hoped to start in November, and thus escape the severities of a British winter, which he felt himself ill prepared to face.

It did indeed seem to Elizabeth, as she drove homeward at a reckless pace that Sunday afternoon, as if life and the world were new again, as if a new force had set the warm blood racing through her veins, as if the very air she breathed had a magical power, and the landscape she looked upon was glorious in the light of a new sun. It was only a little burst of afternoon sunlight, a sudden break in the dull gray sky that beautified the hills, but to her it seemed no common radiance in the skies, no common loveliness in the landscape.

'I would be content to live on just like this for ever,' she thought, 'if I could hear him preach every Sunday.'

Lord Paulyn was enjoying the tardy sunshine before the Gothic porch of Slogh-na-Dyack as his wife drove her ponies up to the chief door of the château. He was smoking a meditative cigar, but not in solitude. His friend Mr. Lampton, a turf magnate, who had exchanged speculation in Manchester soft goods for the more hazardous operations of the turf, was lounging on an adjacent rustic bench, and his toady-in-chief, Mr. Ferdinand Spink, a gentleman who combined a taste for literature with a genius for billiards, supported himself against an angle of the porch, in a state of supreme exhaustion; while seated in a Glastonbury chair within the shelter of the porch appeared the graceful figure of Hilda Disney. It was altogether a pretty domestic picture—the Viscount planted on the threshold of his mansion, his cousin close at hand, his friend and flatterer on either side, like the supporters in the family arms.

'And how little I am wanted here!' thought Elizabeth, with the old feeling of dislike and suspicion about Hilda.

'Been to church?' asked Lord Paulyn coolly.

'Yes.'

'Been doing goody-goody for the lot of us. I'm glad you stick to that sort of thing. It's ballast for the rest of the family.'

'I thought you were going to afternoon church,'

said Elizabeth, turning to Hilda, with a faint suspicion in her look.

'She changed her mind, and stayed at home to talk something over with me,' answered the Viscount. 'She's worth half-a-dozen stewards. I go to Hilda when I want a wrinkle about the management of my estate. She didn't live the best part of her life with such a jolly old screw as my mother for nothing, I can tell you.'

Hilda made no acknowledgment of this dubious compliment.

'Did you like the church at Dunallen?' she asked.

'It is much better than that cast-iron oven.'

Elizabeth's face flamed crimson for a moment as she spoke, the old transient flush like the reflection of evening sunlight. Miss Disney marked the vivid colour, and wondered what there could be in a strange church to call for blushes.

'You had a good sermon, I hope, as a reward for your six miles' drive?'

'Yes,' answered Elizabeth curtly.

She went into the house, passing her husband without so much as a look.

He had Hilda—Hilda's counsel; Hilda, trained in that sordid school at Ashcombe; Hilda, whose genius was to suggest the saving of money. Her bosom swelled with anger and contempt—anger against both, contempt for both.

'Why did he not marry his cousin, and leave me to my lonely life, leave me to be true to the memory of Malcolm Forde?'

She went up to her own room, the room with the stone balcony looking over the water, the soft blue-gray wavelets which flowed beneath the hills that hid Dunallen. How strange, how sweet, how sad to know he was so near her—he from whom she was parted for ever!

'If I had been constant to him, if I had been content to live my blank miserable life in that wretched little house at Hawleigh, to be dragooned by Gertrude, to creep on my dull way like a snail that has never been outside the walls of some dismal old kitchen-garden,—if I had spent all these years in thinking about him and grieving for my loss of his love, would Heaven have rewarded my patience, and brought him back to me at last? Could I by only a little self-denial, only a few years' patience, have been so blessed at last? No; I will not believe it. To think that would drive me mad.'

She sat in the balcony, looking down at the water dreamily, with folded arms resting on the broad stone balustrade, sat living old days over again in a mournful reverie that was not altogether bitter—nay rather perilously sweet, for it brought back the past and the feelings that belonged to the past with a strange reality. Memory opened the gates of a paradise, like that Swedenborgian heaven in which all fairest earthly things have their shadow types. And from the things that had been, her thoughts wandered to the things that might have been—the life she might have lived, had she been true to Malcolm Forde.

'He would have made me a good woman,' she thought; 'and what have I been without him?'

Her newly-awakened conscience reviewed her past life, a career of frivolity and selfishness unleavened by one charitable thought or noble act. She had lived for herself and to please herself, and Heaven, as if in anger, had snatched from her the chosen delight of her selfish soul—the child whose influence might have redeemed her useless life, drawn her world-stained soul heavenward.

Dark was the picture of her life to look back upon; darker still her vision of the future: growing estrangement between her husband and herself—her power lessening daily as her beauty decayed; sinister influences at work to divide them, and on her own part an apathy and disgust which made her shrink from any attempt to retain her hold upon his affection.

The booming of the great gong in the hall below reminded her of the common business of life, but hardly awakened her from her day-dream. She hurried to her dressing-room, and suffered herself to be arrayed for the evening, and went down to the drawing-room, where the Viscount and his friends were dispersed upon the ottomans in all manner of attitudes expressive of extreme prostration, feebly pretending to read newspapers, or look at the pictures in magazines, while they sustained muttered discussions about the odds against this horse, or the chances in favour of that. They made a little pretence of picking themselves up and drawing themselves together at the entrance of Lady Paulyn. Mr. Spink, the literary gentleman, said something funny, in the *Saturday-Review*-and-water style, about Scotch Sabbaths, but, not receiving the faintest encouragement, returned to the study of *Bell's Life* in a state of collapse.

'I don't know what's the matter with her ladyship this evening,' he said afterwards in a burst of confidence, 'but she looks as if she were walking in her sleep.'

Never was sleep-walker less conscious of her surroundings than Elizabeth that night. She performed the duties of her position mechanically; made very fair answers to the inanities which were addressed to her; smiled a faint cold smile now and then; turned the leaves of the book she pretended to read after dinner; caressed the privileged hound, who stretched his long limbs beside her chair and laid his head among the silken folds of her dress, her favourite companion at times, and fondly devoted to her always.

If the strangeness of her manner were evident to the careless eyes of Mr. Spink—a gentleman who considered the universe a clever contrivance designed as a setting for that jewel Spink—it was much more obvious to the eyes of Hilda Disney, eyes that were sharpened by a jealousy which had never slept since the day when Reginald Paulyn first betrayed his admiration for the Vicar's daughter.

What could have happened within the last few hours to bring about so marked a change? That pale set face, those dreary awe-stricken eyes, as of one who had held converse with the very dead—what could these denote?

It was not an edifying Sunday evening by any means. The Scottish underlings of the household shivered as the click of the billiard-balls made itself heard in the servants' hall an hour or two after dinner—but how could the Viscount and his friends have lived through the day without billiards?

Elizabeth looked up from her book after a long reverie, to find herself alone with Hilda in the great empty drawing-room; only they two, sitting ever so far apart, like shipwrecked mariners who had been cast ashore on some desert island, and who were not on speaking terms.

'I hope there is nothing the matter, Lady Paulyn?' said Hilda; 'you are looking so unlike yourself tonight.'

Elizabeth stared at her for a moment doubtfully, with that almost vacant look which had startled Mr. Spink.

'There is nothing the matter—only—only that I am tired of this place!'

'Already? Why, we have been here only a few weeks, and Reginald likes the life so much.'

'That does not oblige me to live here. The place would kill me. I can't endure the solitude. It makes me think too much. I should go mad if I stayed here.'

This from her, who a few hours ago had thanked God for her Scottish home, had deemed it joy and peace unspeakable to breathe the air that was breathed by Malcolm Forde, to live from the beginning to the end of every week cradled in the hope of seeing him for a little while on Sunday! Yes, she had thought all this, but conscience had awakened with much thinking, and she began to feel that even in this delight, which involved no hope of meeting him face to face, of being forgiven, of hearing him speak her name with something of the old tenderness—even in this there was sin. Danger, in the common sense of the word, there could be none, for was not Malcolm Forde as a rock, against whose calm breast the waves of passion beat in vain? But she knew there was peril to her soul in this vicinity; she knew it by the passionate yearning that filled her heart as she sat by this joyless hearth and thought of the life that might have been had she held by her treasure when it was hers to hold, if she had not, at least for a little while, loved earthly pomps and vanities better than Malcolm Forde.

'I can quite imagine that the exertion of thinking must be a new sensation after your life in Park-lane,' said Miss Disney, with her icy sneer; 'but wouldn't it be as well to encourage the habit? The world will hardly be big enough for you if you always run away from thought. And as you grow older, you would find the exercise useful as a way of getting rid of winter evenings. You remember what Talleyrand said to the young man who couldn't play whist? "What a melancholy old age you are preparing for yourself!"'

Elizabeth did not trouble herself to dispute the justice of these observations. She started up from her seat, went over to one of the windows, and flung it open with a sharp decisive action that indicated a mind overwrought. Innumerable stars were shining in the deep dark sky; stars that shone upon him too, she thought, as she looked up at them, with that old, old thought which has thrilled the soul of every man and woman who ever lived, at least once in a lifetime. 'Did he recognise me to-day as I drove past him? does he know that I am near? Does he think of me, and pity me, and regret the foolishness that parted us? O, no; to regret would be sin, and he never sins.'

Lord Paulyn came into the room while his wife was standing at the open window, listening idly to the slow ripple of the waves, looking idly at the glory of the stars, lost in thought; quite unconscious of anything that happened in the room behind her.

He came in alone, languidly yawning. Miss Disney beckoned him over to her, with a somewhat mysterious air.

'What's the matter, Hilda? How confoundedly solemn you look!'

'I am afraid Lady Paulyn is not well.'

'Bosh! She was well enough at dinner. She's been giving herself airs, I suppose. Let her alone, as I do, and she'll come round fast enough.'

'No, no, it's not that. But I really think there is something strange about her. Did you not notice something in the expression of her face at dinner?'

'I have left off watching her looks. I know she's a remarkably handsome woman, and she knows it; and has given herself no end of airs on the strength of her good looks. But there are limits to a man's patience, and my stock of that commodity is very nearly exhausted.'

'Do you remember what you told me about her illness, after the death of your son?'

The Viscount started, frowned, and looked at his cousin with suppressed anger.

'Do you remember telling me that there was a time when the doctors feared that her mind would never recover from that shock?'

'I told you what the doctors said; but the doctors are humbugs. They had a good case, and wanted to make the most of it. I never thought anything of the kind myself. But why the — do you bring this up to-night?'

'Don't be angry. I am only anxious for your sake as well as hers. There is something very strange in her manner to-night. Of course it may mean nothing, only it is my duty to warn you.'

'O, hang duty!' cried Lord Paulyn impatiently. 'I never knew duty urge any one to do anything pleasant. The moment any one mentions duty, I know that I'm in for it.'

He turned upon his heel, paced the room two or three times in an angry mood, and then went out to the balcony, where his wife was standing.

'What are you doing out here star-gazing?' he asked.

The reply came in a softer tone than he was accustomed to hear from Elizabeth's lips.

'I have been thinking a great deal this evening, Reginald, and I am going to ask you a favour. Please don't call me capricious, or be angry with me for asking it; and if you can possibly grant it, pray do.'

'What the deuce do you want?' he asked ungraciously; 'more money, I suppose. You didn't make a clean breast of it the other day when you gave me your bills—though they were heavy enough, in conscience' name.'

'It isn't anything about money. I want you to take me away from this place. I know it is very beautiful. I thought at first I should never be tired of the mountains and the loch, and the sea that lies beyond; but the solitude is killing me. Do let us go away, Reginald, anywhere. I should be happier anywhere than here.'

'I thought as much,' cried Lord Paulyn, with a hard laugh. 'I thought there was some plot hatching between you and Hilda. You'd both like to spread your wings, I daresay. You'd like to go to Paris, or Baden-Baden, or Hombourg, or Brighton. Some nice crowded place, where you could spend money like water. No, my dear Elizabeth, when I brought you here, I brought you here to stay. I know Slogh-na-Dyack isn't lively, but it's healthy, as the doctors all acknowledge, and for the time being it suits me very well indeed. I came here to diminish my expenses, and I mean to stick here till I've filled the hole you dug in my bank balance by your extravagance last season.'

'What!' cried Elizabeth, with ineffable disdain. 'You are here for the sake of hoarding your money! You bring me to this out-of-the-way place in order that I may cost you less! Why don't you send me away altogether? You could save more money that way. I could live upon a hundred a year.'

'Then I am sorry you have never tried the experiment since you have been my wife.'

'Give me back my liberty. Let me go and live somewhere abroad—under a feigned name—alone, my own mistress, free to think my own thoughts, away from this wretched artificial life, which at its best seems to me like acting a part in a stage play. Let me do that, and I will not ask you for a farthing. I will live on the pittance that belongs to me.'

'A very safe offer—even if you meant it, which you don't,' answered Lord Paulyn coolly. 'No, I married you because I was fool enough to be fond of you, and I'm fool enough to be fond of you still. But there comes an end to the period in which a man rather enjoys being twisted round his wife's little finger. I've been pliable enough. I've let you have your full swing. I half suspected when you refused to have anything settled upon you that you meant to spend my money all the more freely, that you didn't want to be limited to a few hundreds, but meant to make ducks and drakes of thousands. I think I've borne with your extravagance pretty well. From this time forward, however, I mean to pull up, and nurse my income, as my mother nursed the Ashcombe estates for me. The three years of my married life have cost me about six times as much as the same amount of time in my bachelor life; and yet I didn't stint myself of any reasonable indulgence, I can assure you.'

'What if I had some special reason for asking you to take me away from this place?' pleaded Elizabeth, without noticing her lord's harangue.

'A woman always has a special reason for wanting her own way,' answered Lord Paulyn, with a sneering laugh.

'So be it,' she said, raising her drooping head and looking at him with flashing eyes. 'I will stay here, then. But remember always that I begged you to take me away, and that you refused me that favour. I will stay here, since you insist upon it, and be happy my own way.'

'Be happy any way you please, so long as you don't worry me with this kind of thing. Come, now, Lizzie, be reasonable, you know. Let us retrench this year, and I'll give you a month or two in Park-lane in the spring. Of course I'm proud of you, and all that sort of thing, and I like to show you off. Only you've contrived to make it so confoundedly expensive.'

'What other happiness do you suppose I expected when I married you, except the pleasure of spending money?' she retorted, in her coldest, hardest tone.

'Upon my soul, you're too bad,' he cried angrily.

'You're not the first woman that has married for money, by a long way, but I should think you're about the first that would look a man in the face and tell him as much without blushing.'

And with this reproach he left her, to go back to his friends and smoke a moody cigar in their congenial society.

CHAPTER VII.

'Henceforth I fly not death, nor would prolong
Life much, bent rather how I may be quit
Fairest and easiest of this cumbrous charge,
Which I must keep till my appointed day
Of rendering up, and patiently attend
My dissolution.'

A STRANGE unrest came upon Elizabeth after that Sunday evening, a slow consuming fever of the mind, which in due course had its effect upon the body. The knowledge of Malcolm Forde's vicinity quickened the beating of her heart by day and night. Her sleep was broken by troubled dreams of their meeting; her days were made anxious by the perpetual question, How soon would accident bring them face to face? Or would he come of his own accord to see her? deeming the past buried deeper than the uttermost deep of a fine lady's memory; come to visit her in his sacred office of priest; come to solicit help for his poor, support for this or that benevolent object; come to make a ceremonious professional call upon the lady of Slogh-na-Dyack.

The days went by and he did not come, and she told herself that she was glad. Yet she kept count of all visitors with a strange watchfulness, and was fluttered by every sound of the bell at the chief doorway. In her walks and drives the same fatal thought pursued her. At every shadow that fell suddenly upon her pathway, at every approaching footstep, she would look up, trembling lest she should see his tall figure between her and the sunlight. Was it a hope that buoyed her up from day to day, or a fear that troubled her? She scarcely dared to ask herself that question.

Sometimes she stayed indoors all day, seized with a conviction or a presentiment that he would come upon that particular day. He would call upon her, and speak gently of that poor dead past, and assure her of his forgiveness, and give her good counsel for the guidance of her life, and teach her how wisely to tread the dangerous path she had chosen. But that day dragged itself slowly out like all the rest, and he did not come.

So passed a week. On Sunday she ordered her pony-carriage, and went to Dunallen, dreading that Miss Disney might offer to accompany her. But the discreet damsel forbore from any such intrusion. She had made her inquiries during the week, and knew perfectly who was officiating, in the absence of the incumbent, at Dunallen Church.

'Your preacher at Dunallen must be much better than ours here,' she said, standing in the porch as Elizabeth passed by to her pony-carriage, 'to tempt you to violate the Scottish Sabbath on two consecutive Sundays.'

'I do not think it any more wicked to drive on a Sunday in Scotland than in Devonshire,' answered Elizabeth.

'Nor I. I was only thinking of the custom of the country. I know at Ashcombe we had a strong inducement to make a long journey to hear your father's curate—that Mr. Forde, who preached such splendid sermons, and seemed always so terribly in earnest. He went to some outlandish place as a missionary, did he not?'

'Yes.'

'What a pity!'

'You need not bewail the fact. He has returned, and is in Scotland. I am going to hear him preach to-day. You can come with me if you like,' answered Elizabeth, with a splendid look of defiance, as much as to say, Whatever sins may stain my soul, they shall not be the paltry sins of deceit and suppression.

'No, thanks. I will come some other Sunday,' said Miss Disney, curiously discomfited by this unexpected candour. She had taken so much trouble, in a secret way, to ascertain the fact which Elizabeth declared so recklessly; not carelessly or indifferently —for her eyes sparkled, and her lips quivered, and the fever flush that had come and gone so often of late reddened her cheek.

Miss Disney had a spare half-hour before the morning service at the iron chapel, leisure in which to pace slowly to and fro upon the lawn before the Norman Gothic porch, thinking of her cousin and her cousin's wife.

Did she seriously mean to injure either of them, or deliberately plot the ruin of her fortunate rival? No. Nor had she any thought of a day when death might sweep that rival from her path, and she herself be Lady Paulyn. She knew her cousin Reginald too well to hope for that; knew that his brief fancy for her had never been more than an idle man's caprice, and had perished utterly ten years ago; knew that whatever wealth of affection he had to bestow he had squandered upon his wife; knew that there was no farther outcome of feeling to be hoped for from his selfish soul—that whatever love he could feel, whatever self-sacrifice he was capable of, love and sacrifice alike would be wasted upon Elizabeth. She hoped nothing therefore, had no scheme, no dream; only stood by like the Chorus in an old tragedy, or prophesied to herself, like a mute Cassandra.

But she had loved her cousin—had in that distant, unforgotten day cherished her golden dream of a happy prosperous existence to be spent by his side—and she could not see him quite as he really was, in all the utter commonness of his nature.

As for her feelings towards Elizabeth—well, it was hardly to be supposed that she should love the woman who had stolen from her that crown of life which she herself had hoped to wear—the woman who, after having robbed her of this treasure, scarcely took the trouble to be civil to her. No, she did not love her cousin's wife.

'What shall I do?' she thought, as she walked to and fro; 'I can understand the change in her now—the change which only began last Sunday afternoon. It was the shock of seeing this man again. And she goes to-day to hear him preach, and will contrive to see him perhaps after the service. What ought I to do? Warn my cousin that his wife's old lover is living within a few miles of him, or hold my tongue and let him make the discovery for himself? He is sure to make it, sooner or later, and I do not owe him so much devotion that I need put myself in a false position to save him a little trouble.'

So Miss Disney did nothing, and suffered matters to take their course, contemplating the situation in a cynical spirit, prepared for anything that might happen. It seemed as if the old dowager's gloomy prophecies—and she had prophesied about the various evils to come of her son's marriage with the convulsive fury of a pythoness on her tripod—were in a fair way to be realised.

'It really seems hardly worth while to hate anybody actively,' mused Miss Disney, 'for the people one dislikes generally manage to do themselves the worst injury that malice could wish them, sooner or later.'

This Sunday was finer than the last. The autumn sun shone with rare splendour, the little church at Dunallen was full to over-flowing. The word had gone forth throughout the neighbourhood that Mr. Mackenzie's substitute was a fine preacher, a man who had done good service as a missionary, too. People had come from a long distance to hear him. Elizabeth felt herself a unit among the crowd. There was no fear that he would be disturbed by the sight of her, she thought; yet she had a seat tolerably near the pulpit—the pew-opener having been eager to do her honour—a seat at the end of an open bench in a diagonal line with the preacher.

How sweet a sound had the familiar prayers when he read them! what a sound of long ago!—full of old sad memories of the churches at Hawleigh, and her dead father's kindly face. They filled her soul with tenderness and remorse. How wicked she had been all her life! how hard, how selfish! She was not fit to worship among his flock. How many and many a time, Sunday after Sunday, her lips had gabbled those prayers mechanically, while her worldly thoughts were wandering far away from the fane where she knelt! It seemed as if his voice gave a new meaning to the old words; stirred her soul to its profoundest depth, as the pool was troubled at Siloam. Not for a long while—hardly since her girlhood, when she had had fitful moments of religious enthusiasm in the midst of her frivolity—had she felt the same fervour, blended with such deep humility. All the fever and excitement of the last week was lulled to rest in the solemn quiet of that little church among the hills. Again she felt that it was enough for her to be near this saintly teacher, whom she had once loved with but too earthly a passion; enough to be near him, and that she might be good for his sake—a better wife even.

'I will try to do my duty to my husband,' she said to herself, as she sat listening to the sermon her eyes bent on the open book in her lap, not daring to look up, lest his eyes should meet hers; strangely dreading that first direct look—the stern recognising gaze of those dark eyes of his—after this gap of time.

His sermon was upon duty. A straight and simple discourse, adorned by no florid eloquence, but made touching by many a tender allusion to that lovely life which is the type aud pattern of all human excellence. He spoke of the duties which belong to every relation of life; of children and of parents, of husbands and of wives. It was a sermon after the apostolic model; friendly counsel to his new friends, here among remote Scottish hills, away from the falsehoods and artificialities of crowded cities; a simple pastoral address to the people of this small Arcadia.

'If I could only obey him!' Elizabeth thought; at this moment a different creature from the brilliant mistress of the house with the many balconies—the presiding genius of crowded afternoon tea-drinkings, the connoisseur in ceramic ware, who would melt down a small fortune into a service of eggshell Sèvres, or Vienna, or Carl Theodore cups and saucers, and cream-jugs and tea-canisters, for the mere amusement of an idle morning; a widely different being from her whose last ball had astonished the town by its reckless extravagance, whose milliner's bill would have been formidable for Miss Killmansegg.

By nature a creature of impulse, carried away by every vain wind of doctrine, she was at least accessible to good influences as well as evil, and was for this one brief hour exalted, purified in spirit by the power of her old lover's pleading—pleading not as *her* lover, only as one who loved all weak and erring human creatures, and had compassion unawares for her.

'Does he know?' she wondered; 'does he know that I hear him? Surely he must have cast one of his penetrating glances this way.'

Nothing in his tone or manner indicated the surprise or emotion which might have accompanied such a recognition. If he had seen her the sight had not moved him, the memories which shook her soul to its centre had no power to touch him. He was like rock. She remembered the old bitter cry that had gone up from her lips in those dreary days when she had waited for his coming back to her—

'His heart is stone!'

Strange that a heart should be so tender for all mankind, yet so hard for her.

'There was a time when I thought my love was worth any man's having, just because they told me I was prettier than other women. Yet *he* has shown me that he could live without it, that he could have it and hold it, and let it go without a pang.'

Not once during the half-hour in which he spoke to his listening flock had she dared lift her eyes to his face. Sweet though it was to hear him, it was almost a relief when the sermon ended. She breathed more freely, stole one little look at the pulpit where he knelt, saw the dark head and strong hands clasped before it, and wondered again if he knew that she was so near. Then came the chink-chink of the sixpences, the gradual melting away of the congregation, and she was standing before the Gothic doorway. This time Donald did not keep her waiting. The carriage was ready for her. She drove home very slowly, still wondering.

CHAPTER VIII.

'Thou hear'st the winter wind and weet,
　　Nae star blinks through the driving sleet;
Tak' pity on my weary feet,
　　And shield me frae the rain, jo.

The bitter blast that round me blaws
　　Unheeded howls, unheeded fa's:
The cauldness o' thy heart's the cause
　　Of a' my grief and pain, jo.'

LORD PAULYN left Scotland in the following week, to go to Liverpool, where there were races being run in the early autumn; and his friends departed with him, to be replaced by a relay of other friends when he returned to Slogh-na-Dyack—a return which was at present problematical. There were a good many races crowded together at this 'back end' of the year: a late regatta at Havre, where Lord Paulyn had pledged himself to sail his yacht, the Pixy; races at Newmarket, at Pontefract, at the Curragh of Kildare, in all which events his lordship was more or less interested.

So the two ladies were left alone in the Norman château, to sit in the long tapestried drawing-room, with its modern antiquities, a kind of Brummagem Abbotsford collection, which had filled the soul of the knife-powder manufacturer with pride during his brief occupation of his castle. They were alone, and were fain to stay indoors for the greater part of the week, during which period there was rain ; such rain as does at times bedew Scotia's fair countenance; rain persevering, rain incessant, cloud above cloud piled Pelion-upon-Ossa-wise on the mountain-top, and discharging torrents of water. Every tiny watercourse upon the hill-side, a narrow thread of silver in fair seasons, was broadened to a small cataract ; every lowland river overflowed its rugged banks, and brawled and blustered over its stony bed, with a turbulent air, as if some long-imprisoned spirit of the stream had broken suddenly loose and were eager to make havoc of the country-side.

Very long and dreary seemed those rainy autumn days to the mistress of the château and her uncongenial companion. Elizabeth secluded herself in her own rooms, and tried to read, or tried to draw, or tried to find a tranquillising influence in her piano,— a Broadwood, with a sweet human tone in its music ; a tone that answered to the touch of the player, and was not all things to all men, after the fashion of some newer and more brilliant instruments. She played for hours at a time—played out her sorrows, her brief flashes of joy, which were at most the joys of memory, her moments of exaltation, her intervals of despair—played and was comforted, or laid her head upon the piano and wept soothing tears. She had nothing human on this earth to love; the life that she had chosen for herself left her outside those small tepid loves or likings which are the *pis-aller* of less self-contained spirits. Even the thought of Blanche, her favourite sister, in these moments of despair, inspired only a shudder. She loved her dog better than anything else in the world—except that one person of whom only to think was a sin—and the dog, being dumb, seemed to sympathise with her, or at least never uttered trite commonplaces in the way of consolation, but looked up at her with dark solemn loving eyes, and seemed to be moved with human pity, when she wept upon his broad honest head.

At last there came a break in the sky; the clouds upon the hill-tops rolled away, and disclosed the blue heaven whose face they had veiled so long; the cheerful sunshine brightened the waters; cornfields and green pastures on the shores of Bute ceased to be blotted out by the inexorable rain. The world was born again, as when Noah's ark came aground on the topmost peak of Ararat. The occasional fine days of a Scotch summer are apt to be very fine, and this last glimpse of summer's splendour crowning the brow of autumn was bright and glorious.

Elizabeth was somewhat cheered by this change in the weather. It gave her at least liberty.

Nor was she slow to avail herself of this recovered freedom. Long before noon she was on the hills beyond sight of Slogh-na-Dyack. Those heathery slopes and narrow footpaths by which she went were swampy after the long rains, and wide water-pools lay in every hollow, like polished steel mirrors reflecting the high blue sky; but it is no longer one of the characteristics of a fine lady to take her walks abroad shod in satin slippers, and Elizabeth stepped through mud and swamp with a fearless tread, in her comfortable mountain boots. O sweet autumn breezes, O lovely world! if one could only be satisfied with the delight of mountain scenery, and wide blue lakes sleeping in the rare sunshine!

That week of rain seemed actually to have exhausted the evil propensities of the Caledonian atmosphere; one fine day succeeded another, days whose serenity was only disturbed by half-a-dozen or so of showers or an occasional tempest of hail; and Elizabeth—who defied brief showers, and even transient hailstorms, or the sudden obscuring of the heavens behind a curtain of black clouds, presage of a passing hurricane—wandered about the mountains in delicious freedom, and seemed almost to walk down the demon of despondency and the sharp stings of remorse. She rarely drove, for she could hardly use her pony-carriage without offering Miss Disney the spare seat at her side, and she loved best to be alone, quite alone, without even Donald the gillie seated behind her, open-mouthed and empty-headed, staring vacantly at the sky.

She liked to climb the hill-side alone, to wander alone among the sheep, who were seldom scared by her light footstep, or to sit upon some craggy bank, where fragments of primeval rock seemed to be mixed up with the heather and the short mountain grass, as if this part of the world had but just emerged, inchoate and unfinished, from chaos. She loved to sit here alone, her sealskin jacket drawn tightly across her chest, defying the autumnal winds, in whose sweet freshness there was a sharp sting now and then, like a faint prophecy of coming winter. Here she had time for sad thoughts, time to repent the foolishness of all her life gone by, and to long, with how vain a longing, that the past could be undone.

Sometimes, as she walked homeward in the

beginning of the dusk, foolish fancies would steal into her mind at sight of the white towers and pinnacles of Slogh-na-Dyack rising above the evening mists at the base of the mountain—the thought of what her life would have been if she and Malcolm Forde had inhabited that northern château; how every room in that great house would have been brightened and glorified by domestic love; how sweet to go home from her walks to be welcomed by him; how sweet to stand in the porch at eventide watching for his coming—vain, useless fancies, which consumed her heart; fancies which she knew to be sinful even, but could not put out of her mind.

Thus passed the second week of Lord Paulyn's absence, and there was as yet no hint of his return. Elizabeth was still free to live her own life, a life of utter loneliness, the life of a woman who lived in the past rather than in the present; free to wander among those solitary hills, with the dog Gregarach for her only companion.

Wide and varied as had been her wanderings, she had never yet crossed the path of Malcolm Forde. She had almost left off hoping for or dreading any such encounter. Had she chosen to put herself in his way, to take the village of Dunallen in the course of her rambles, or to loiter among the outlying cottages that sprinkled the hill-side just around the village, she would have been very sure to meet him. But this was just the one thing which Elizabeth, in her right mind, could not do. Nor, had she languished to behold him as the fever-parched wayfarer in a dry land languishes for a draught of cold water, could she have deliberately waylaid him. She knew that to think of him was wrong, yet she thought of him by day and by night, having long lost the empire over her thoughts. But she was still the mistress of her actions, and could keep them pure.

She made the most of the fine weather, however, without coming too near Dunallen; and even when there came threatenings of a change, menacing clouds again brooding over the mountain peaks, she was not alarmed, and left Slogh-na-Dyack as usual, immediately after breakfast, with the faithful Gregarach at her side.

'You are not going out to-day, surely,' said Miss Disney, who had come down to the hall to consult the barometer; 'the glass has gone back to much rain.'

'I thought we ought to have screwed the hand to that particular point the week before last,' answered Elizabeth; 'much rain seemed to be the normal condition of Scotland. Yes, I am going for my constitutional. I daresay I shall have a shower, but I'm used to that.'

'I'm afraid you'll have a storm, and there's not much chance of shelter among those hills. It's really very wrong of you to run such risks.'

'The risk of catching cold, for instance,' said Elizabeth contemptuously. 'I never catch cold. I sometimes think I have a charmed life, unassailable by the elements.'

'You are very lucky, in that particular as well as in so many others. I can scarcely put my head out of doors on a damp day without paying for my imprudence with neuralgia or influenza.'

'How disagreeable!' said Elizabeth, looking at her absently. 'Come, Gregarach.'

She walked rapidly away, under the dull threatening sky, leaving Hilda in the porch, looking after her thoughtfully.

'What a miserable restless creature she is, in spite of her prosperity!' she said to herself. 'One ought hardly to envy her. Does she ever meet her old lover on those lonely hills, I wonder? No, I scarcely think that. He is not the kind of man to run any hazard of scorching his wings at the old flame, and she—well, no, I do not believe she is bad enough for that. She only wanders about because she is discontented, and still madly in love with the man who jilted her.'

Two hours later those ominous clouds upon the mountain resolved themselves to rain, a dense driving rain that came down like a sheet of water, and threatened to extinguish the landscape in watery darkness. Miss Disney stood at one of the drawing-room windows watching the deluge.

'Good heavens, if she is without shelter in such rain as this!' she thought, not without compassion. 'What is to become of her?' And then, with a cynical bitterness, 'If she were to catch her death of cold it would be very little advantage to me. What is that some poet says?—"Even in their ashes lurk their wonted fires." But some ashes are quite cold. *Nothing* would rekindle *them*.'

On the hill-tops that blinding rain made a worse darkness, a confusion of sound as it came sweeping down with a shrill whistling noise, like the wind shrieking in the shrouds at sea, while ever and anon came the hoarse roar of distant thunder, shaking, or seeming to shake, even those deep-rooted hills. Elizabeth stood beneath the tempest, looking helplessly about her, the dog cowering at her side, wondering what she should do. She was very indifferent to small inconveniences in the way of weather, but this was a tempest which threatened to sweep her off the mountain-side, to whirl her into the teeth of the welkin, unsubstantial and helpless as a tuft of thistledown. Even Gregarach, the deerhound, who should have been accustomed to this war of the elements, shuddered and was afraid.

'If there were a cave, or anything of that kind, handy,' she said to herself, trying to look through the rain. She might as well have tried to pierce the curtain of futurity itself. The world was a thing expunged; there was nothing left but herself, her dog, and the deluge.

'The barometer was right for once in a way,' she said. 'This is "much rain." But I thought barometers were things one ought to read backwards, like gipsy women's fortune-telling.'

Happily she was not unfamiliar with her surroundings, and could hardly go astray or topple over a precipice unawares. She had roamed the mountain too often for that in her two months of residence at Slogh-na-Dyack. She stood quite still, pondering, while the pitiless rain drenched her garments, reducing even the comfortable sealskin to a black shiny-looking substance, from which the water ran, not as from a duck's back, but soaking the fabric thoroughly as it trickled slowly down.

What should she do? where seek her nearest

shelter? Yes, she bethought herself at last of a place of refuge at the base of the lonely hill-side on which she stood, a refuge so insignificant that it had hardly impressed its image on her memory, though she had looked down upon it many a time from this very spot; an object which, in her dire distress to-day, came back to her indistinctly, with a kind of uncertainty, as a thing which might be real or only an invention of her own fancy.

'Yes,' she thought, 'I do believe there is one solitary cottage down there, at the very foot of this hill. I have a vague recollection of seeing it, and a thin thread of smoke curling up from its poor little chimney, a miserable shanty of a place, with grass growing ever so high on the roof; but O, what a comfort it would be to find myself under a roof of any kind just now! Come, Gregarach, old fellow, we'll make for the cottage.'

It was hard work getting down the steep mountain-side in that blinding rain. She had held up her little silk umbrella as well as she could against the violence of the wind—she had now to furl it and make it her staff. Her feet slipped upon the sodden grass more than once during the slow descent, and for the moment she fancied it was all over with her, and she must roll down to the valley, bruised and beaten to death in her swift course. 'Such a nasty dirty death!' she thought, with a shudder.

But the firm light feet kept their vantage-ground, the slender figure held itself erect against the buffeting of the wind and the force of the raindrift, and Lady Paulyn arrived finally, only half-drowned, in the narrow road at the base of the mountain—a lonely cheerless road at the best of times, skirted by a rocky bank, beneath which ran a deep narrow stream, now swollen to the width of a small river—a spot that was eminently unattractive except from the artistic and Salvator-Rosa point of view—a region of sterility and gloom, which hopeless grief might choose for its abode, where nature seemed in unison with man's despair, where the braes never bloomed and the birds never sang.

Yes, there was the cottage, 'just a but and a ben;' grass growing high upon the steeply sloping roof, the tiny square window obscured by a handful of hay stuffed into one broken pane and a fragment of linsey-woolsey in another. The very abode of desolation, but still a roof to cover one, Elizabeth thought gladly.

The door was shut. She knocked, but no one came; then tried the latch, and opened the door and peered in, an action which even in that moment of extremity brought back the thought of the old days at Hawleigh, when she had stood at cottage doors with so light a heart, so full of vague hope and unacknowledged love.

'May I come in?' she asked gently, unable to see whether the place were occupied, so profound was the obscurity within. Her dog emphasised the question by a fortissimo bark.

Even that loud inquiry brought no reply. 'The place must be empty,' thought Elizabeth, and made bold to enter, Gregarach going before her with loud sniffings and a suspicious air.

The little wretched room was unoccupied, but there was some poor apology for furniture in it. A chest of drawers—article most dear to the Scottish mind—a battered old table and one chair, a few odds and ends of crockery on a shelf in a corner, and a good deal of dirt. There were signs of occupation, too; a struggling turf fire on the hearth, and beside the fire an old black saucepan containing some herby decoction, from which came a faintly aromatic odour.

'Odd,' thought Elizabeth, 'but I suppose the people are out at work. Poor creatures, I wonder what work they can find to do in such weather as this.'

She took off her jacket, which seemed a mere mass of brown pulp; took off her hat, also sealskin reduced to the same pulpy condition; and tried to shake off a little of the water which hung in every fold of her garments. She tried to put a little more life into the turf fire, to get something like heat out of it if possible, but it was only a lukewarm fire, and she looked about the room in vain for more turf or a fagot of wood.

'What a wretched place!' she said to herself; 'and to think that some poor creature will come here for comfort by and by when his work is done—is thinking of it now, perhaps, and longing for it, and calling it *home*.'

She thought of Slogh-na-Dyack, her own suite of rooms, with their many windows looking over the water, the infinite luxury, the triumph of man's inventiveness exemplified in every contrivance that can make life pleasant; she thought of the dismal contrast between this home and hers, and of her own discontented mind, to which that costly château had seemed no better than a splendid prison.

'Why cannot fine scenery and handsome furniture satisfy one's heart?' she said to herself. 'Why must one always long for something else, for some one whose mere presence would make such a shelter as this tolerable, for some one in whose company one would have no thought of worldly wealth or worldly pleasure?'

She looked round the darksome little room — looked up at the low broken ceiling, which was rain-blistered and stained — looked round with a sad smile.

'If Malcolm had married me, and poverty had reduced us to such a place as this, I would have been happy with him,' she thought. 'I would have tucked up my sleeves and scrubbed and toiled, and tried to make this wretched hovel bright and comfortable for him. It would have been my pride to bear deprivation, misery even, for his sake. I could then have said to him, "You doubted me once, Malcolm, but is not *this* real love?"'

She had seated herself in the solitary chair close by the low open hearth, trying to get a little warmth out of the fading fire, trying not to shiver very much with that wretched sensation of cold and dampness which had crept over her since she had found shelter in the cottage. She had opened the door two or three times and looked out, with a faint hope of seeing some indication of fair weather, or at least some lessening of the rain; but the water-drops came down with a sullen persistence—came down as she had seen them fall day after day from her window, without a break in the watery monotony.

'I wonder if I shall have to stay here two or three days,' she thought, 'while all the Slogh-na-Dyack people are searching the country for me, and a private detective watching all outward-bound vessels that leave the Clyde, lest I should have taken it in my head to run away to America? It really seems as if I should have to choose between staying here all day and all night, or walking home in the wet. If I could only see a stray boy—a native boy inured to rain—I might send him home for a carriage.'

But looking for stray boys seemed almost as hopeless as watching for the ending of the rain; so Elizabeth shut the door, and went back to the dismal hearth, which became every minute colder and more dismal, and to her own sad useless thoughts.

She was startled from her reverie presently by a sudden activity on the part of Gregarach, who had been quiet enough hitherto, having stretched himself among the ashes, in the hope of getting warm, where he had lain until now, dozing fitfully, and looking up at his mistress wistfully ever and anon, as who should say, 'We might surely have found better quarters.'

Now he started to his feet, gave his short bark,

like the sergeant's cry of 'Attention!' and ran to the door communicating with the other chamber of the cottage; a darksome little den, into which Elizabeth had looked when she first took shelter; a room which had seemed to her utterly empty. The door was a little way ajar; the dog pushed it open with his nose, and rushed in.

Elizabeth started up, not frightened—fear and Elizabeth Luttrell had ever been strangers—only anxious; while there flashed across her brain old stories of Scottish shelters, and faithful dogs, whose sagacity had protected their masters from murder.

'I have my watch and purse,' she thought, 'and all these foolish diamond rings, which I put on my fingers every morning from sheer habit, just as a red Indian tricks himself out with beads and wampum. I should be rather a valuable booty. And this cottage has an uncanny look at the best of times, standing alone, under the shadow of the hill, and with that deep dark river running yonder, ready to swallow up murdered travellers.'

She was not frightened, though it was not beyond the scope of possibility that this vision, conjured up half in jest, might be realised in hideous earnest. That sad and bitter smile, so frequent on her lips of late, lighted up her face just now, as she thought how such things have been, and how lives more precious than hers had come to dark and terrible ending.

How well that swift river could keep a secret! It would be so easy a matter to dispose of her. The dog might give a little trouble, perhaps, but a knock on the head would make an end of him, and what resistance could *she* offer? Then would follow a long and tedious quest; rewards offered, heaven and earth moved, as it were, on behalf of a lady of quality, but the mystery for ever unsolved. Dark scandals invented perhaps; her reputation tarnished by foul imaginations. Some people preferring the belief that she was living a shameful secret life somewhere, to the simpler theory of her untimely death.

She could almost fancy what society would say of her in years to come, when her husband had married again and forgotten her.

'O, there was another Lady Paulyn, you know, who disappeared in a curious manner. No one knows whether she is alive or dead; but Lord Paulyn married again, all the same—his cousin—a Miss Disney, a much more suitable match. The first wife was a very pretty woman, gave capital parties, and so on; but they did not live happily together.'

And *he* would hear of her dark fate, and wonder,

and be sorry. Yes, surely even his stony heart would be moved by her dismal end; that most horrible of all dooms, at least to the minds of the survivors, the fate about which there is uncertainty.

She had time for all these thoughts while Gregarach was sniffing about the inner room.

Presently he set up a piteous whine; whereupon Elizabeth, with a calm fixed face, as of one who goes to her doom, pushed the door open again—it had swung to behind the dog—and went boldly into the gloomy den, where murder perchance lurked in the shawdow of the sloping roof.

The dog was standing with his forepaws upon a miserable little bed; a bed she had not observed in her first inspection of the chamber; a bed set into the wall, cupboard fashion, after the manner of some Scottish beds, the lower end inclosed by a wooden shutter, the head sheltered by a checked blue curtain, limp and ragged.

A withered skinny hand grasped this meagre drapery,—hardly the hand of a stalwart assassin; a hand of a dirty waxen hue, wasted by age or sickness, —and a feeble voice entreated plaintively, 'Tak' awa' the dog.'

Elizabeth ran to the bed. 'Don't be frightened, he won't hurt you,' she said. 'Down, Gregarach;

down, old fellow. Indeed you needn't be afraid of him; he's a sensible affectionate fellow.'

The dog licked his mistress's hand, as if in grateful acknowledgment of this praise. She had as yet seen no more of the occupant of the bed than that skinny hand clutching the curtain; but the curtain was drawn back now, revealing a ghastly figure; a woman, old, or made prematurely old by toil and care and sickness; a face haggard as death itself, under a tumbled nightcap; dim eyes staring at the intruder with vague wonder.

'Something to drink,' gasped this helpless creature; 'for God's sake give me something—the stuff that auld Becky made.'

Elizabeth looked round her helplessly. She could see no sign of a cooling draught for those pale parched lips; not even a pitcher of water, much less the stuff concocted by old Becky, whoever that person might be.

'O, where shall I find you something?' she said. 'Poor soul, I'll do anything in the world for you, if you'll tell me how.'

'The stuff by the fire,' said the woman; 'but dinna leave yon doggie with me.'

The stuff by the fire; that dark concoction in the saucepan. The recollection of it flashed upon Elizabeth. She called her dog, and went back to the outer room; found a cracked mug, poured some of the dark-looking drink into it, and carried it back to the sick woman, and held it gently to the dry lips, supporting the weary head upon her arm, with a touch of that natural tenderness which had endeared her to the cottagers at Hawleigh.

'Have you been long ill?' she asked.

'Three weary weeks. I've keepit my bed three weeks, but I was bad before; all my limbs aching, and a weight on my head. I could hardly keep about to do for myself and my son; he's a farm labourer, beyond Dunallen; and then I was forced to give up, and tak' to my bed. The fever's been mickle bad about these parts.'

'The fever!' repeated Elizabeth, with a faint shiver, but not any shrinking motion of the arm that supported the sick woman's head.

'Yes, it's been verra bad; maybe you shouldna be in here; some folks call it catching, but I dinna ken. The Lord knows where I could have caught it, for there's few folks come my way to bring me so much as a fever, except the new minister. I suppose you're the minister's wife?'

Elizabeth smiled at the question. 'No,' she said, 'I'm not the minister's wife. It was only selfishness that brought me here; I was caught in the storm, and came to your cottage for shelter. But now I am here I may be able to help to get you well. I can send you wine, and tea, jelly, broth, all kinds of things to strengthen you. And a doctor, too, if you've had no doctor.'

'I've had auld Becky, she kens as much as ony doctor; and the new minister, he knows a deal. And he brings me wine and things, but it's very little that I can tak' the noo, I'm so low. There's some wine in yon cupboard; you might gie me a drappie.'

'Let me settle your pillow more comfortably first.'

She arranged the pillow, fever-tainted perhaps; the whole chamber had a faint fœtid odour that tried her sorely. But fear of death, even in this den, where lurked a foe scarce less deadly than the assassin of her imagination, she had none. The day was past when her life had been worth cherishing. She placed the pillow under the weary head, wiped the damp brow with her handkerchief, murmured a few comforting words, phrases she had learned in the brief period of her ministrations, and then went to the cupboard, a little hutch in a corner, to seek for the wine.

The new minister; that was he, no doubt. She

touched the bottle almost reverently, thinking that his hand had sanctified it. The woman hardly put her lips to the cup; it was only by gentle entreatings that Elizabeth could induce her to take a few spoonfuls of the wine. Not all the vintages of Oporto could have brought back life or vigour to that worn-out habitation of clay, in which the soul fluttered feebly, before departing for ever.

There was a Bible on a chair by the shuttered end of the bed.

'Will you read me a chapter?' asked the woman, after an interval of feeble groanings and muttered lamentations.

Elizabeth opened the book immediately, chose that chapter of chapters, that tender farewell address of Christ to his Apostles, the fourteenth of St. John, and began to read in her low earnest voice, as she had read many a time in the sunny cottages at Hawleigh, with the bees humming in the myrtle-bushes outside the window, the green trees waving gently under the summer sky. This gloomy hovel in the shadow of the mountain seemed a bit of another world.

She read on till the patient sank into an uneasy slumber, breathing heavily. And then, seeing her to all appearance fast asleep, Elizabeth laid the book down, and looked at her watch. It was nearly five o'clock; the day, which had been dark at two, was growing darker; the rain, which she could just see through the cloudy glass of the narrow casement, was still coming down steadily, with no symptom of abatement.

'It is clear I shall have no alternative between walking home in the rain or staying here all night,' thought Elizabeth. 'Or, stay: this poor soul spoke of her son; he will come home by and by, perhaps, and he might fetch the carriage for me.'

There was comfort in this hope. Though not afraid of the fever, she was not a little desirous to escape from that tainted atmosphere, in which to breathe was discomfort. And yet it seemed cruel to leave that helpless creature, perhaps to die alone.

'I must try to find a nurse for her, somehow,' she thought; 'I'll ask her about this old Becky when she wakes. It seems almost inhuman to let her lie here alone.'

She wondered that Malcolm Forde had not done more for this stricken creature. But there were doubtless many such in his flock, and he had done his utmost in bringing her wine and coming to see her now and then.

The woman had been asleep about half-an-hour,

while Elizabeth sat and watched her, thinking her own sad thoughts, when the outer door was opened. It was the son returning from his work, no doubt. Elizabeth rose, and went to meet him, anxious to have tidings of her whereabouts conveyed to Sloghna-Dyack before nightfall.

She had her hand upon the door between the two rooms, when another hand pushed it gently open. Drawing back a little, she found herself face to face with Malcolm Forde.

She could see, plainly enough, that for the first few moments he failed to recognise her in the halflight of that dismal chamber. He looked at her, first in simple wonder, then with eager scrutiny.

'Good God,' he cried at last, 'is it *you* ?'

'Yes,' she answered, with a feeble attempt to take things lightly. 'Did you not know we were such near neighbours ? Strange, isn't it, how people are drawn together from all the ends of the earth, Parthians and Medes and Elamites, and the dwellers in Mesopotamia ?'

He seemed hardly to hear her. He was looking at the bed, with an expression of unspeakable horror.

'Come into the next room,' he said, drawing her quickly across the threshold, and shutting the door upon the sick chamber. 'What brought you to this place?'

'Accident. I came here to find shelter from the rain.'

'You had better have stayed in the rain. But God grant that you may have taken no harm! I come here daily, and stay beside that poor creature's bed for an hour at a time. But I believe custom has made me fever-proof. You must get home instantly, Lady Paulyn; and take all possible precautions against infection. That woman has a fever which may be—which I fear is—contagious; but I trust in God that your superb health may defy contagion, if you are only reasonably careful.'

He opened the outer door to its widest extent. 'Let us have as much air as we can, even if we have some rain with it,' he said. 'It is too wet for you to go home on foot. I must find some one to run to Slogh-na-Dyack and fetch your carriage.'

'You know where I live, then?' with a wounded air. It seemed so stony-hearted of him to be quite familiar with the fact of her vicinity, and yet never to have broken down the barriers of reserve, never to have approached her in his sacred character. To be careful for all the rest of his flock, for all the other sinners in this world—Fiji islanders even—and to have not one thought, not one care, no touch of pity for her!

'Yes,' he answered, in his cool grave way, imperturbable as the very rock, looking at his watch thoughtfully. 'The young man will not be home till seven perhaps. I must go to Slogh-na-Dyack myself.'

'What, through this rain! O, please don't. You'll catch your death of cold.'

'I came here through this rain, and I am very well protected,' he said, glancing at his mackintosh. 'Yes, that is the only way. Promise me that you will stand at this open door till your carriage comes for you.'

'But if that poor soul should call me, if she should be thirsty again, I can't refuse to attend to her, can I, Mr. Forde?'

'What, you have been attending to her—hanging over her to give her drink?' with a look of intense pain.

'Yes; I have been arranging her bed a little, and giving her some wine you brought, and doing what I could to make her comfortable. It reminds me of—of the old time at Hawleigh, when I had a short attack of benevolence. O, please don't look so anxious. I am sure not to catch the fever. What is that line of somebody's?—"Death shuns the wretch who fain the blow would meet." I am just the kind of useless person who never dies of anything but extreme old age. You will see me creeping round Hyde Park, forty years hence, in a yellow chariot and a poke bonnet, with pug-dogs and a vinegar-faced companion.'

'You have not left off your old random talk,' he said regretfully. 'I cannot forbid you to obey the dictates of humanity. If the poor old woman should ask you for anything, you must give it. But do not bend over her more than you can help, and do not stay in that room longer than is absolutely necessary. I have arranged with a woman at Dunallen to come and nurse her. She will be here to-night.'

'I am glad of that, and I shall be still more glad if you will let me contribute to your poor. May I send you a cheque to-morrow?'

'You may send me as many cheques as you like. And now, good-bye. The carriage will be here before I can return.'

He gave her his hand, with an air so frank and friendly that it stung her almost as if it had been an insult, pressed the little ice-cold hand she gave him in his friendly clasp, and went out into the rain.

'He never, never, never could have loved me,' she said to herself, looking after him with a piteous face, and bursting into a passion of tears. What had she expected? That he, Malcolm Forde, the man who had given his life to God's service, would fall on his knees at the feet of Lord Paulyn's wife, in the surprise of that sudden meeting, and tell her how she had broken his heart five years ago, and how she was still much more dear to him than honour, or the love of God?

'He looked frightened at the idea of my having caught the fever,' she thought, when she had recovered from that foolish burst of passionate anger, bitter disappointment, unreasoning and unreasonable love. 'But that was only from a philanthropic point of view; just as a family doctor would have done. Was there ever any one so impenetrable? One would think we had never been more than the most commonplace acquaintance, and had only parted from each other a week ago.'

She stood leaning against the door-post, looking at the dreary waste of sodden turf, the fast-flowing river, the mountain on the other side of the valley, which was like a twin brother of the mountain behind the cottage.

She stood thus, lost in gloomy thought, thought that was more gloomy than the landscape, more monotonous than the rain, when a footstep sounded a little way off. She looked up and saw Mr. Forde coming back to her.

'I met a lad who was able to carry the message faster than I could,' he said, 'so I have returned, to prevent your running any risk by ministering to that poor soul yonder.'

He looked into the other room; the woman was still asleep. He waited a little by the bed-side, and then came back to the doorway where Elizabeth stood looking out at the turbid water.

'How long is it since you were caught in the rain?' he asked—a foolish question, perhaps, inasmuch as it had rained without ceasing for the last four hours.

'I hardly know; it seems an age. I was wandering about the mountain for ever so long, not knowing what to do, till I happened to remember this cottage, and then we came down, my poor drenched dog and I, and crept in here for refuge. And I seem to have been here half a lifetime.'

Half a lifetime, more than a lifetime, she thought; for were not the joys and sorrows of any common existence concentrated in this meeting with him? The dog was licking his hand, with abject affection, as if he too had known this man years ago, and been parted from him, and loved him passionately throughout that severance; but strange creatures of the dog-tribe had a habit of attaching themselves to Mr. Forde.

'And you have been in your wet clothes all this time,' he said anxiously, with the pastor's grave solicitude, not the lover's alarm. 'I fear you may suffer for this unfortunate business.'

'Rheumatism, or sciatica, or lumbago, or something of that kind,' she said; 'those seem such old woman's complaints. I daresay I shall have a fearful attack of rheumatism, and my doctor and I will call it neuralgia, out of politeness. No one on the right side of thirty would own to rheumatism.' This, with her lightest good-society manner.

'I should recommend you to send for your doctor directly you get home, and take precautionary measures.'

'I have no doctor,' she answered, a little impatiently; 'I hate doctors. They could not save the child I loved—and—' Her lip quivered, and the dark beautiful eyes filled, but she brushed away the tears quickly, deeply ashamed of that confession of weakness.

'You have lost a child?' said Mr. Forde; 'I heard nothing of that. I know very little of the history of my old friends since I left England. I did hear of your dear father's death, and was deeply grieved, but I have heard little more of those I knew at Hawleigh.'

Not a word of her marriage; but he had heard of that, no doubt; had heard and had felt no surprise, taking it for granted that she was engaged to Lord Paulyn when he set forth upon his mission.

'I am sincerely sorry to hear you have lost one so dear to you. But God, who saw fit to take your little one away, may, in his good time—'

'Please do not say that to me. I know what you are going to say; it has been said to me so often, and it only makes me more miserable. I could never love another child as I loved him, the one who was snatched away from me just when he was growing brighter and lovelier every day. I could never trust myself to love another child. I would keep it a stranger to my heart. I would take pains to keep it at a distance from me. I should think it a dishonour to my dead boy to love any other child. But don't let us speak of him. I have been forbidden ever to speak or to think of him.'

'Forbidden? By whom?'

'By the doctors. I don't know what made me speak of him just now. It is like letting loose a flood of poisoned waters.'

He looked at her gravely, wonderingly, with a

look of unspeakable sorrow. Was it for this she had broken faith with him? Had all the splendours and vanities of the world brought her so little joy? The wan and sunken cheek, the too brilliant eye, told of a heart ill at ease, of a life that was not peace.

'Let us talk of yourself,' she said, in an eager hurried manner. 'I hope you found the life—about which you had dreamed so long—a realisation of your brightest visions?'

'Yes,' he answered with a far-off look, which of old had always suggested to Elizabeth that she was of very small account in his life. 'Yes, I have not been disappointed; God has been very good to me. I go back to my work at the close of this year, and to work in a wider field.'

'You go back again, back again to that strange world!' with a faint shudder. 'How little you can care for your life, and for all that makes life worth having!'

'For life itself, for the bare privilege of existence in this particular world, I do not care very much; but I should like to be permitted to finish my work, so far as one man can finish his allotted portion of so vast a work.'

'And the savages,' said Elizabeth, 'did they never try to kill you?'

'No,' he answered, smiling at her look of terror. 'Before they could quite make up their minds to do that, I had taught them to love me.'

'And you will go out to them again, and die there! For if they spare you, fever will strike you down, perhaps, or the sea swallow you up alive in some horrible shipwreck. How can you be so cruel—to yourself?'

'Cruel to myself in choosing a pathway that has already led me to happiness, or at least to supreme content!'

'Supreme content! What, you had nothing to regret in that dreary, dreary world? O, I know that it is full of flowers and splendid tropical foliage, and roofed over with blue skies, and lighted by larger stars, and washed by greener waves, than we ever see here; but it must be so dreary—twelve thousand miles from everything.'

'From Bond-street, and the Burlington-arcade, and the Royal Academy, and the opera-houses,' said Mr. Forde, as if he had been talking to a wayward child.

'Do you think I am not tired enough of those things and this world?' she cried passionately. 'Why do you speak to me as if I were a baby that had never cut open the parchment of its toy-drum to find out where the noise came from? I asked you a question just now. Had you nothing to regret in your South-Sea islands?'

'Nothing, except my own worldly nature, which still clung to the things of earth.'

She looked at him curiously, wondering whether she was one of those things of earth for which his weak soul had hankered. His perfect coolness was beyond measure exasperating to her. It was not that she for one moment ignored the fact that for those two there could be no such thing as friendship —no sweet communion of soul with soul, secure from all peril of earthly passion, in that calm region where love has never entered. She knew that this accidental meeting was a thing not to be repeated without hazard to her peace in this world and the next, or to such poor semblance of peace as was still hers. Yet she was angry with him for his placid smile, his friendly anxiety for her welfare, the quiet tones that had never faltered since he first greeted her, the grave eyes that looked at her with such passionless kindliness. If he had said to her, 'Elizabeth, I have never ceased to love you—we must meet no more upon this earth '—she would have been content; but, as it was, she stood looking moodily down at the angry river, dyed red with the clay from its rugged banks, telling herself over and over again that he had never loved her, that he was altogether adamant.

Being a woman, and not a woman strong in the power of self-government, she could not long devour her heart in silence. The wayward reckless spirit sought a relief in words, however foolish.

'You do not even ask me if I am happy,' she said, 'or how I prospered after your desertion of me.'

'Desertion!' he echoed, with a short laugh; 'women have a curious way of misstating facts. My desertion of you! Desertion is a good word. Forgive me for not having inquired after your happiness, Lady Paulyn. I had a right to suppose that you were as happy as every woman ought to be who has deliberately chosen her own lot in life. I trust the choice in your case was a fortunate one.'

'I had no choice,' she answered, in a dull despairing tone, looking at the river, not daring to look at him. 'I had no choice. I went the way Fate drifted me, as helpless or as indifferent as that tangle of weeds yonder, carried headlong down the stream. I was miserable at home with my sisters; so, thinking any kind of life must be better than the life I led with them, I married. I have no right to complain of my marriage; it has given me all the things I used to fancy I cared about, long ago, when I was a vain silly girl; nor have I any right to complain of my husband, for he has been much better to me than I have ever been to him.'

'Why do you palter with the truth?' he cried sternly, turning upon her with an angrier look than she had seen in his face, even on the day when they parted. 'Why do you try to disguise plain facts, and to deceive me, even now? What pleasure can it give you to fool me just once more? What do you mean by being drifted into your marriage, or why pretend that you married Lord Paulyn because you were miserable at home? You were engaged to him before you left your aunt's house. You were married to him as soon as my back was turned.'

'That is false!' cried Elizabeth. 'I was not engaged to him till you had left England.'

'What, he was not your accepted lover when I saw you in Eaton-place—when I showed you that newspaper?'

'He was not. The newspaper and you were both wrong. I had refused Lord Paulyn twice. The last rejection took place the night before that morning, the night of the private theatricals at the Rancho.'

She held her head high now, the sweet lips curved in a scornful smile, proud of her folly—proud, even though she had wrecked her own life, and had perchance shadowed his, by that very foolishness.

'And you suffered me to think you the basest of women—to surrender that which was dearer to me than my very life—only because you were too proud to tell me the truth!'

'Would you have believed if I had told you? I don't think you would. You had judged me beforehand. You would hardly let me speak. You believed a printed lie rather than my piteous looks—the love that had almost offered itself to you unasked that night at Hawleigh. You could think that a woman who loved you like that would change in two little months—could be tempted away from you by the love of rank and money. I never thought that you could leave me like that. I was sure that you would come back to me. O God, how I waited and watched for your coming! how I hated those fine sunshiny rooms in Eaton-place which saw my misery! And then when I went back to Hawleigh, thinking I *might* see you again, perhaps, and you *might* forgive me, I was just in time to hear your farewell sermon. And when I went to your lodgings the next morning, to beg for your forgiveness—yes, I wanted you to forgive me before you left us all for ever—I was just too late to see you. Fate was adverse once more. The train had carried you away.'

'You went to my lodgings!' he exclaimed, with breathless intensity. 'You would have asked me to forgive you, me, the blind besotted fool who had been duped by his own passion! You loved me well enough to have done that, Elizabeth!'

'I would have kissed the dust at your feet. There is no humiliation I could have deemed too great if I could have only won your forgiveness; not won your love back again—the hope of that had no place in my heart.'

'My love!' he said, with a bitter smile. 'When did that ever cease to be yours?'

Her whole face changed as he spoke, glorified by the greatness of her joy. He had loved her once—and that once had been for ever!

But not long did passion hold Malcolm Forde in its thrall. He felt the foolishness of his words so soon as they had been uttered.

'It is worse than idle to speak of these things now,' he said. 'If I wronged you by a groundless accusation, you wronged me still more deeply by withholding the truth. That day changed the colour of our lives. Of my life I can only say that it is the life to which I had long aspired, which I would have sacrificed for no lesser reason than my love for you. It has fully satisfied my desires. I will not say there have been no thorns in my path, only that it is a path from which no earthly temptation could now withdraw me. For yourself, Lady Paulyn, I can only trust—as I shall pray in many a prayer in the days to come, when we two shall be on opposite sides of the world—that your life may be filled with all the blessings which Heaven reserves for those who strive to make the best use of earthly advantages.'

'You mean that having made a wretched mistake in my marriage, and having lost the child who made life bright for me, I am to console myself by church-going and district-visiting, and by seeing my name in the subscription list of every charity.'

'The field is very wide,' he said, every trace of passion gone from voice and manner. 'You need not be restricted to a conventional rôle. There are innumerable modes of helping one's fellow creatures, and no one need despair of originality in well-doing.'

'It is not in me,' she answered wearily. 'And if I were ever so inclined to help my fellow creatures, my opportunities henceforward are likely to be limited. I have been guilty of culpable extravagance; it is so difficult to calculate the expense of what one does in society, and I never was good at mental arithmetic.

In plain words, I have made my husband angry by the amount of my bills, and I shall henceforward have very little money at my command.'

'I should have supposed that Lady Paulyn's pin-money would be ample fund for benevolence, which need not always be costly,' said Mr. Forde, conceiving this self-abasement to be merely a mode of excusing her disinclination for a life of usefulness.

'I have no pin-money,' she answered carelessly. 'I refused to have a settlement. When a woman marries as much above her as I did, there is always an idea of sale and barter. I would not have the price set down in the bond.'

'Your husband will no doubt remember that generous refusal when he has recovered from any vexation your unthinking extravagance may have caused him.'

'I don't know. We have a knack of saying disagreeable things to each other. I have not much indulgence to expect from him. Do you ever pass our house at Slogh-na-Dyack?'

'Sometimes.'

'Sometimes,' she thought, with exceeding bitterness; and he had never been tempted to cross the threshold, never constrained, in his own despite, as passion would constrain a man who could feel, to enter the house in which she lived, to see with his own eyes whether she was happy or miserable.

'And yet he talks of having never ceased to love me,' she said to herself.

Then resuming her old light tone—the tone that had so often jarred upon his ear in the bygone time —she said,

'When next you pass Slogh-na-Dyack, think of me as a prisoner inside those high white walls, a prisoner looking out at the water, and envying the white-sailed ships that are sailing round Cantyre, the seagulls flying over the hills. It is a very fine house, and I have everything in it that a reasonable woman could desire; but I feel that it is my prison, somehow.'

'How do you mean?'

'Lord Paulyn has brought me here to retrench. He is a millionaire, I believe, but millionaires are not fond of spending money, and, as I told you just now, I have spent his with both hands. Pray don't think that I am complaining, only—only, when you go past my house, think of me as a solitary prisoner within its walls, and pity me if you can.'

The assumed lightness was all gone now, and in its stead came piteous tones of appeal.

'Pity you!' he cried passionately. 'Are you trying to find out the quickest way to break my heart? You had always a knack at playing with hearts. Elizabeth, do not speak to me any more. Pity me. I am weaker than water. Why do you not tell me that you are happy—that the world, and the pleasures and triumphs of the world, are all-sufficient for you? Why do you wish to distract my soul by these suggestions of misery? And to-night, perhaps, amongst your friends, you will be all life and brightness—a creature of smiles and sunshine—as you were in the play that night.'

'I can act still,' she said, with a faint laugh. 'But it is too much trouble to do that at Slogh-na-Dyack. I have no friends there; it is a hermitage, without the peace of mind that can make a hermitage pleasant. Don't look at me so sorrowfully. I shall go back to London, I daresay, in the spring, if I am good, and shall give parties, and spend more money, while you are among your Fiji islánders.'

Malcolm Forde answered nothing, but stood with a gloomy brow staring at the rushing water. What a shallow nature it seemed, this soul of the girl he had loved once and for ever; what a childish perversity and capriciousness, and yet what dreary suggestions there were in all her talk of a depth of misery lurking below this seeming lightness! Ah, what torture to part from her thus, knowing nothing of what her life was like in the present, what it might become in the future; knowing only that it was not peace, and that all those loftier hopes and nobler dreams which had sustained him in the darkest hours of his existence were to her a dead letter!

They kept silence, both watching that dark and turbid river, almost as if it had been that river in the under world by which they must each stand one day, waiting for the grim ferryman. But in a little while the sound of wheels mingled with the noise of the water,—wheels and horses' feet approaching swiftly on the wet mountain road.

'Thank God!' said Mr. Forde; 'the carriage at last. How you shiver! I must beg of you to remember what I have said about taking prompt means to ward off the cold, and it would be as well to take some precautionary steps against infection: not that I fear any danger from that,' he added hopefully. Then, looking at her with undisguised tenderness— for was it not, as he believed, his very last look?— 'Elizabeth, I shall pray for you all my life. If the prayers of any other than yourself can give you peace and good thoughts and a happy life, you will never lack those blessings. Good-bye.'

He held her hand for a little while, looking at her

with those dark searching eyes which she had feared even before she loved him; looking through her very soul, trying to pierce the thin veil of pretence, to fathom the mystery within. But even at the last she was a mystery too deep for his plummet-line.

'Good-bye,' she said, and not one word more, remembering that other parting, when, if speech could have come out of her stubborn lips, she might have kept him all her life. What could she say now except good-bye?

He put her into the dainty little brougham, wrapped her in the soft folds of a fur-lined carriage-rug, gave the coachman strict injunctions to drive home as fast as his horses would safely carry him, and then stood bare-headed at the cottage-door watching her departure.

CHAPTER IX.

'My God! I never knew what the mad felt
Before; for I am mad beyond all doubt!
No, I am dead! These putrifying limbs
Shut round and sepulchre the panting soul,
Which would burst forth into the wandering air.
What hideous thought was that I had e'en now?
'Tis gone; and yet its burden remains here,
O'er these dull eyes—upon this weary heart!
O world! O life! O day! O misery!
*   *   *   *   *   *
She is the madhouse nurse who tends on me.
It is a piteous office.'

WHETHER a careful compliance with Mr. Forde's behest would have saved Elizabeth from the evil consequences of that one wet day, it is impossible to say. She took no precautions; she was utterly reckless of her own safety, hating doctors and all medical appliances with a childish hatred, and never from her childhood upwards having cared to take any trouble about herself in the way of preserving her health. That health had hitherto been a splendid inheritance which recklessness could hardly reduce. She had run wild in Devonian woods wet-footed, and caring no more for the damps of morass or brooklet than a young fawn; she had roamed the moor in the very teeth of the east wind, had lingered latest of all the household in the vicarage-garden when the heavy night-dews were falling; she had sat up late into the nights reading her favourite books, had existed for weeks at a time with the least possible allowance of sleep, and had hardly known what it was to be ill.

'I almost wish I could set up a chronic headache like Diana's,' she used to say in those days. 'It is so convenient occasionally.'

But after her boy's death had come an illness which concentrated into nine long weeks of anguish more than some feeble souls suffer in a lifetime of weak murmurings and complainings. Brain-fever, it would have been called most likely, had the patient been any one less than Lord Paulyn's wife; but the specialists, who met three times a week in solemn conclave to discuss the diagnostics of the case, found occult names for the ailments of a person of quality. That nameless fever of mind and body, engendered of a wild and desperate grief, came and passed away; but not without severely trying the strength of the mind, which had been the greater sufferer. The inexhaustible riches of a superb constitution saved the body, but that weaker vessel the mind foundered, and at one time was menaced with total shipwreck.

Now fever again took possession of that lovely temple—the lowest form of contagious fever—and rang its dismal changes from gastric to typhus, from typhus to typhoid. Wet garments, tainted air, did their fatal work. After a week or so of general depression, occasional shivering fits, utter want of appetite, and continued sleeplessness, the fever-fiend revealed himself in a more definite form; and the local surgeon—resident five miles from the château—declared, with infinite hesitation and unwillingness, that in his opinion Lady Paulyn was suffering from a mild form—a very mild form, and entirely without danger—of the low fever that had been hanging about the neighbourhood this year.

This declaration was made, in the most cautious and conciliating manner, to Lady Paulyn herself, in the presence of Hilda Disney; the disagreeable fact disguised with an excessive show of confidence and hopefulness on the doctor's part, just as he contrived to conceal the flavour of aloes or rhubarb in his silvered pills.

Elizabeth turned her haggard fever-bright eyes to him with a strange look. She had been sitting in a moody attitude till now, staring fixedly at the ground.

'I have had fever before,' she said; 'and that time my mind went. I could not believe it for long afterwards, but I know now that it did go. I hope that is not going to happen to me again.'

'My dear lady,'—Elizabeth shuddered; the specialists, or in other words mad-doctors, had always called her 'dear lady,'—'there is not the smallest cause for such an apprehension. In fever there is occasionally a slight delirium, purely attributable to physical causes. But I trust that with care there may be nothing of the kind in your case.'

'With care!' repeated Elizabeth. 'Yes, I remember they said that when I was ill before. I heard them, as I lay there helpless, repeating the same words every day like parrots. But then I only wanted to die, and to go to my darling; and I don't know that it matters much more now. Only I don't want to lose my mind, and yet go on living. If I am to die young, let me die altogether, not like Dean Swift, first a-top.'

The Scotch surgeon, an eminently practical man, shook his head a little at this, with a grave sideglance at Miss Disney; then murmured his directions: quiet—repose—the saline draughts, which he would alter a little from those of yesterday and the day before—and, above all, care. It would be as well to send to Glasgow for a professional nurse, lest the duties of the sick-room might be beyond the scope of Miss Disney or Lady Paulyn's maid. This was mentioned in confidence to Hilda when she and the surgeon had left Elizabeth's room together.

'It is not going to be serious, I hope,' said Hilda.

'I apprehend not. No; I venture to think not. With youth, and so fine a constitution—no organic disease—I have every reason to imagine the fever will pass off in a few days, and a complete restoration ensue. But the want of sleep and of appetite are unpleasant symptoms, and her ladyship's mind is more excited than I should wish. I think, as it is a case which no doubt will inspire some anxiety in the mind of Lord Paulyn, and as he is absent from home, it might be wise to fortify ourselves with a second opinion.' This was said with an air of proud humility, as who should say, 'I feel myself strong enough to cope with the diseases of a nation, but usage must be observed, according to the statute in such case made and provided;' for medicine has its unwritten laws, its unregistered acts of an intangible parliament. 'I should like Dr. Sauchiehall to see Lady Paulyn.'

'Pray telegraph to him at once,' said Hilda anxiously; 'and I will telegraph to my cousin.'

With this understanding they parted. The doctor to drive his neat gig to the little bathing-place five miles off, whence he could send a telegram to Glasgow; Hilda to pace the terrace, under a gray autumn sky, watching, or seeming to watch, the white rain mists rolling up from the mountain crests, and meditating this new turn in affairs.

How would Reginald take his wife's illness? They had parted with a palpable coolness; on her part indifference, smothered anger on his. Would all his old selfish vehement love rush back upon him with redoubled force if he found his wife in jeopardy? Such hours of peril, as it were the shadow of the destroyer lurking on the threshold of a half-opened door, are apt to awaken dormant affections; to rekindle passions that seemed dead as death itself.

'I know that he loves her still,' thought Hilda. 'Those flashes of anger spring from the same root as tender looks and sweet words; he loves her still, with quite as much real affection, and as near an approach to unselfishness as he is capable of feeling. And if she were to die—he would never love any one else; would marry again perhaps, but for money, no doubt, the second time. And I—well, I should be always in the same position, a miserable hanger-on, outside his life. God give me patience to do my duty to both of them; to the man who amused a summer holiday by breaking my heart, and the woman who has usurped my place in the world.'

To communicate by telegraph or post with Lord Paulyn was no easy matter, or there was at least small security that a telegram would find him. His address was fugitive; at Newmarket to-day, on board his yacht in Southampton Water, bound for Havre, to-morrow. Hilda telegraphed to Newmarket and Park-lane, trusting that one of the two messages might reach him without delay. She also wrote him a letter, addressed to Park-lane, in which she gave him a careful account of Elizabeth's symptoms, and the medical man's remarks upon them. Having done this she felt that she had done her duty, and could abide the issue of events with a complacent mind.

But a harder and more painful duty remained to be done; the patient had to be watched and cared for, and that task Miss Disney deemed herself, in a manner, bound to perform. A horrible restlessness had taken possession of Elizabeth. Weak as she was, she wanted to roam from room to room, out on to the lonely lawn even, under the dull gray sky; and Mr. McKnockie, the local surgeon, had especially directed that she should be kept in perfect quiet, and in her own room—that she should straightway take to her bed, indeed, and, as it were, prostrate herself at the feet of the fever fiend.

Against this Elizabeth protested with all her might, declaring that she was not ill, that she had nothing the matter with her but cold and sore-throat, and that Mr. McKnockie was only trying how long a bill he could run up with his vapid tasteless medicines. Air, fresh air, was all she required, she cried; and she flung open the French window, and went out into the balcony, in spite of Hilda.

'O sea, sea, sea,' she cried, looking away towards that opening in the hills where the waters widened out into ocean, 'if you would only carry me away to some new world, a world of dreams and shadows, where I should have done with the burden of life!'

Alas, she was only too near that world of dreams and shadows! Before nightfall she was delirious, watched over by hired nurses, a prostrate wretch concerning whom the doctors Sauchiehall and McKnockie shook their heads almost despondently. Fever of mind and fever of body raged together with unabating violence. She had entered the region of dreams and shadows; and in that long delirium, during which all things in the present were blotted out, or only seen dimly athwart a thick cloud, her mind went back to the past. She was a child again, following the windings of the Tabar, or losing herself in the wood where the anemones were like snow in April; she was a girl again, her childish unspoken love for Malcolm Forde ripening slowly, like a bud that ripens to a blossom under a gentle English sun, until it bursts into bloom and beauty, the perfect flower of woman's heart.

In that drama of the past which she lived over again, there were not only scenes that had been, but scenes that had not been. With the loss of sober reason and the perception of surrounding things, invention was curiously quickened. Memory, which was beyond measure vivid, ran a race with imagination. That brief span of her springtide courtship, the few short weeks of her engagement to Malcolm Forde, were spun out by innumerable fancies of the distracted brain. She recalled walks that they had never walked, long wanderings over the moor; wild poetic talk; the converse of spirits which had issued forth from the doors of this solid world into a vast cloudland, a place of dim unfinished thoughts and broken fancies.

It was distracting to hear her talk of these things; it was a madness almost maddening to watch or listen to. The hired nurses made light enough of the business; haled their patient about with their coarse hands, tied her even with bonds when she was too restless for their endurance; ate, drank, slept, and rejoiced, while she lay there in her dream-world, entreating Malcolm to loosen those cruel cords, to take her away out of the stifling atmosphere that was killing her.

Miss Disney made a point of spending some hours of the day or night in the sick-room; and in these hours Elizabeth fared a little better than at other times. The tying process was at any rate not attempted in Hilda's presence. But, consciousness of all immediate events being in abeyance, the hapless patient knew not that she was being protected by this quiet figure in a black-silk gown, which sat statue-like by the hearth, and she was exceedingly tormented by the sight of it. In her more desperate moods she even accused Miss Disney of keeping her a prisoner in that horrible room, and of separating her from her plighted lover.

Here was one of the mental obliquities which made a part of her disorder. Her husband and her married life, even her lost child, were forgotten; were as things that had never been. Nothing stood between her and her first lover, except the bondage that kept her to that hated room. He was at all times close at hand, waiting for her, calling to her even, only she could not go to him. Every creature who held her back from him was her enemy; and chief among these, the despotic mistress of her prison-house, the arbiter of her fate, was Hilda Disney.

Matters were in this state when Lord Paulyn came back to Slogh-na-Dyack, tardily apprised of his wife's illness by the telegrams, which had followed him from stage to stage of his wandering existence. He found the doctors at sea, only able to give stately utterance to the feeblest opinions, but by a curious fatality issuing orders which in every minutest detail were opposed to the desires of the patient.

In her more lucid intervals she had languished for the sight of old faces, the sound of old voices. She had entreated them to send for the old servant who had nursed her, the old vicarage servant who had been part-and-parcel of her home in the happy childish days before her mother's death, before she had begun to be proud of her beauty and to grow indifferent to the commonplace present in selfish dreams of a much brighter future. She spoke of the woman by her name, remembering all about her with a singular precision, at which the doctors looked at each other, and wondered; 'Memory extraordinarily clear,' they remarked, like heaven-gifted seers divining a fact which it was not within the power of common perception to discover.

Then came a longing for her sisters, above all for Blanche, the young frivolous creature who had loved her better than she had ever loved in return. Piteously, in her most reasonable moments, she implored that Blanche might be summoned.

'She would amuse me,' she said, 'and I want so much to be amused; all is so dull here, such an awful quiet, like a house under a spell. For heaven's sake, if there is any one in this place who loves me, or pities me, let them send for my sister Blanche.'

Miss Disney, faithful to her duties in a semi-mechanical way, informed the medical men of this wish.

'Would it not be well to send for Miss Luttrell?'

No, they said. Isolation — perfect isolation — offered the only chance of recovery. Lady Paulyn was to see no one except the persons who nursed her. No old familiar faces—inspiring violent emotions, agitating thoughts — were to approach her. Even Miss Disney, who might be permitted to take her turn occasionally in the patient's room, must be careful not to talk to her—not to encourage anything like conversation. Soothing silence must pervade the chamber — sepulchral as the room where the mighty dead lie in state. When Lord Paulyn came, he might see his wife, but with such precautions as must reduce any meeting between them to a nullity. The dismal monotony of a sick-room was to be Elizabeth's curé; the hard cruel visages of hireling nurses were to woo her back to reason and peace: so said Dr. Sauchiehall, Mr. McKnockie, as in duty bound, agreeing.

Lord Paulyn came at a time when mere bodily illness had been well-nigh subjugated, and that nicer mechanism, the mind, alone remained out of gear. He was allowed to stand for a few minutes in the shadow of the curtains that draped his wife's bed; and having the misfortune to come in an unlucky hour, heard her rave about her first lover, and upbraid the tyrants who had severed them. He turned upon his heel, and left the room without a word; nor did he enter again until, upon a terrible occasion, some weeks later, when the malady had increased—even under those favourable circumstances of utter isolation and the care of hireling nurses—and he was summoned to his wife's room to prevent her flinging herself out of the window by the sheer force of his strong arm.

She was clinging to the long French window when he went into the room—an awful white-robed figure with streaming hair and flashing passionate eyes, the two nurses trying to drag her back, but vainly striving against the unnatural strength that waits upon a mind distraught.

'Why do you keep me back from him?' she cried. 'He is down yonder by the water waiting for me, as he has waited always. I heard his voice just now. You shall not keep me back. Do you think I am afraid of the danger? At the worst it is only death. let me go.'

Lord Paulyn's strong arm thrust the nurses aside, grasped the frail figure, whose convulsive force was strangled in that muscular grip. She struggled with him, and was hurt in the struggle—hurt by the grasp of that broad hand, which seemed so brutal in its strength. She looked at him with her wild fever-bright eyes.

'I know you now,' she said; 'you are my husband. The other was a sweet sad dream. You are the bitter reality!'

He flung her into the arms of the head nurse—a virago six feet high. 'If you cannot take better care of your patient, I must have her put where they will know how to look after her without boring me,' he said; and left the room without another look at the only woman he had ever loved. There are some flames that burn themselves out very soon, the fierce love of selfish souls among them. The warmth of

Lord Paulyn's affection for his wife had long been on the wane. Her extravagances had tried his temper, touching him deeply where he was most susceptible, in his love of money. Her illness had annoyed him, for he detested the fuss and trouble of domestic affliction. This second calamity struck a final blow to his self-love, with which was bound up whatever yet remained of that other love. That her wandering mind should set up 'that parson fellow' in his rightful place—should erase him, Reginald Paulyn, from the story of her life—harking back to that old foolish sentimental passion of her girlhood, was too deep an offence.

He sat by his lonely hearth, and brooded over his wrongs—his wife's base ingratitude, his childlessness—hardly daring to look forward to the future, in which he saw the creature he had once loved menaced with the direst affliction humanity can suffer. He summoned the mad-doctors—the men who had taken out a kind of patent for the manipulation of the distraught mind—the men who had called Elizabeth 'dear lady,' a year ago, in Park-lane. They came, and agreed in polite language, which shirked the actual word, that Lady Paulyn was very mad; they feared hopelessly, permanently mad. Nature, of course, had vast resources, they added, sagely providing for the event of her recovery—there was no knowing what healing balm she might ultimately produce from her inexhaustible storehouse—but in the mean time there could be no doubt of the main fact, that her ladyship was suffering from acute mania, and must be placed under fitting restraint.

There was a little discussion as to which of the doctors should have the privilege of ministering to this amiable sufferer. One had a charming place— an old-fashioned mansion of the Grange order in Surrey; the other a handsome establishment on the north side of London. They debated this little matter between themselves, like polite vultures haggling about a piece of carrion, perhaps drew lots for the patient, and finally arranged everything with an air of agreeable cordiality. The physician whose house was in the north had won the day.

'You must contrive to get me through any formalities that may be necessary as easily as you can,' said Lord Paulyn. 'It's a horrible business, and the sooner it's over the better. Poor thing! She was the loveliest woman in England, bar none, when I married her. I feel as if we were committing a murder.'

'Be assured, my dear sir, that the dear lady could not be more happily placed than with our good friend Dr. Cameron,' said Dr. Turnam, the gentleman who had resigned the prey to his brother patentee. 'If skill and care can restore her, rely upon it they will not be wanting.'

The Viscount sighed, and went back to his solitary smoking-room, breathing muttered curses against destiny. She had worn out his love; but to think of her handed over to this doctor—consigned, perhaps, to a life-long imprisonment—*that* was hard. What should he do with himself, when she who had made the glory of his life was walled up in that living grave? He had Newmarket still, and his stables; and at his best he had given more of his life to the stable than to Elizabeth. But he felt not the less that his life was broken—that he could never again be the man that he had been; that even the hoarse roar of the ring and the public when his colours came to the front in a great race would henceforth fall flat upon his ear.

CHAPTER X.

> ' Yes, it was love, if thoughts of tenderness
> Tried in temptation, strongest by distress,
> Unmov'd by absence, firm in every clime,
> And yet, O! more than all!—untir'd by time;
> Which naught remov'd, nor menac'd to remove—
> If there be love in mortals, *this* was love.'

A GLOOM fell upon the spirit of Malcolm Forde after that meeting in the sick woman's cottage. The thoughts of his old life, his old hopes, bright dreams of union with the woman he fondly loved, pleasant visions of a simple pastoral English life among people it would be his happiness to render happy, a fair prospect which he had cherished for a little while, only to lose it by and by in bitterness and disappointment—the thoughts of these things came back to him and took the sweetness out of his pleasant existence, and made all the future barren.

It was hard to know that he had his own impetuosity to blame for the ruin of his earthly happiness; harder to be content remembering how he had been permitted to realise that other and unselfish dream of carrying light to those that sat in darkness; hard to say, 'Lord, I thank Thee; Thou knowest best what is good for me; Thou hast given me far more than I deserve.'

Not yet could his spirit soar into this holy region of perpetual peace; a region where sorrows are not, only mild chastenings of a heavenly Master, who leavens every affliction with the leaven of faith and hope. His thoughts were of the earth, earthy. His mind went back to that day in Eaton-place, and he hated himself for his unreasoning anger, for the false pride which would not let him court an explanation; for his blind passion, which had taken the show of things for their reality.

He thought of what might have been if, instead of casting away this flower of his life on the first indignant impulse of his jealous mind, he had shown a little patience, a little tenderness. But he had seemed incapable of patience on that odious day; with his own angry foot he had kicked down the air-built castle which it had been so sweet to him to raise.

If he had found her happy, serene in the glory of her high position, secure in the sympathy and affection of a worthy husband, he would not have felt his own loss so keenly; he could have borne even to know that she had never loved him better than in that luckless hour when he renounced her. But to know that her life had been shipwrecked by his mad anger—to look into her haggard face, with its sad mocking smile, and know that she was miserable—to read the old love in those lovely eyes, the old love cherished always, confessed too late by unconscious looks that pierced his very soul—these things were indeed bitter.

For a while he forgot his profession; forgot what he was, and the work that still remained for him to do; sank from his lofty level of self-renouncement to the lowest depths of a too human despair. If the image of his lost love had haunted him in that strange romantic world amid the waters of the Pacific, how much more did that sad shade pursue him now, when the woman he still loved was near at hand, when from the hill-side which he had daily need to pass he could see the white walls of the house she had called her prison!

Never more might his eyes search the secrets of that altered face—the face which he remembered in all the pride of its girlish beauty. Never any more might those two meet. To all other world-weary souls he might carry consolation, might breathe words of promise and of hope; but not to her. Between them rose the barrier of a mighty love, unconquered and unconquerable.

He went his quiet way with that great sorrow in his heart. Had he not carried almost as great a sorrow even in the islands of the southern sea? only that he had then regarded his loss as inevitable, while he now lamented it as the wretched fruit of his own fatuity. He went his quiet way and did the little there was to be done in that scantily-peopled district, visited the sick, comforted the dying; but the work he did just now was done in a semi-mechanical way, for his heart was elsewhither.

It would have been a relief to him if he could only have heard of her; if there had been any one who could tell him how she fared. He looked at the white walls, the conical towers, longingly, yet would not go near them. To enter there would be to enter the gates of hell. But he would have risked much to hear of her.

His eyes searched the little chapel at every service, but saw her not. Yet this might augur nothing except that she instinctively avoided him, with an avoidance he must needs approve.

Weeks passed, and he heard nothing; and that mountain scene seemed strangely blank to him, as if that one figure, met only once, had filled the whole landscape. Then came a day upon which duty took him near Slogh-na-Dyack. He went to see a sick child in a cottage within half-a-mile of the château; and here, almost by accident, he first heard of Lady Paulyn's illness.

He had asked the boy's mother if she had everything necessary for him; everything the doctor had ordered. Yes, she told him, they got everything from the big house where the poor lady was so ill.

He had been bending tenderly over the fever-stricken child, but he looked suddenly upward at these words.

'What house? what lady?' he asked quickly.

'The house with the peaky lums,' the woman answered. 'Lady Paulyn, who took the fever, and is lying ill with it still; near death, some folks say.'

He laid the sick boy gently down upon his pillow, and then questioned the woman closely. She could tell him no more than she had told him in that one sentence. The lady at Slogh-na-Dyack had been dangerously ill; the doctors came there every day: a doctor from Glasgow, and another doctor from Ellensbridge. Some said she was dying; but she had lain sick so long, and hadn't died, so there was hopes of her getting well. The fever had been quicker with poor bodies like hersen. It was a good many weeks now since Lady Paulyn had been took.

What could he do? He left the cottage, and walked straight to Slogh-na-Dyack, with no definite idea as to what he should do, only that he would at least discover for himself how far the woman at the cottage had been right. Those people always exaggerate; pick up wild versions of common facts. Elizabeth might have been ill, perhaps, but not dangerously. He tried to persuade himself this as he walked swiftly along the misty road.

He did not stop to consider his right, or want of right, to approach her. Such an hour as this made an end to all such questions. If she were dying, it was his duty to be near her; to sustain that poor weak soul, of whose mystery he knew more than any other man on earth. By his right as a minister of God's word and her dead father's friend, he would claim the privilege of being near her at the last dark hour.

The land in front of the château looked gray and gloomy in the twilight, the darkness only broken by the red light of a wood fire in the hall. A pompous butler, imported from Park-lane, and sorely averse to this Northern establishment, was basking in a Glastonbury chair before the cavernous fireplace, yesterday's *Times* lying across his knees, to-day's *Scotsman* and *Edinburgh Daily Review* crumpled into the corner of the chair; the seneschal having dropped comfortably off to sleep after exhausting the news of the day.

Disturbed by the entrance of Malcolm Forde, this functionary rose from his slumbers, and imperiously commanded an underling to light the gas, 'which is about the honly convenience we 'av in this detestable barracks of a place,' he was wont to say, 'and 'av to make it ourselves in the kitchen-garding, at the risk of being blowed out of our beds.'

Questioned by Mr. Forde, this personage affirmed that Lady Paulyn was ill, very ill; but not in any danger. She had been in danger three weeks ago, when the fever was at its height; but there was no danger now.

'Yet you say that she is still very ill.'

'Very ill, sir; leastways, she keeps her own room; but is, I believe, progressing towards convoluscence. Would you wish to see Miss Disney, sir? Lord Paulyn have gone to Hinverness for a few days' deer stalking, but Miss Disney is at home.'

'No; if you can assure me that Lady Paulyn is out of danger, I need not trouble Miss Disney. But in the event of danger, I should be very glad if that lady would send for me. You can give her my card. I am an old friend of Lady Paulyn's family.'

He gave the butler his card, and went away relieved, but still uneasy.

How gloomy the house looked! The dark oak staircase, with its mediæval newels; the Scottish lion rampant, supporting the shield of the knife-powder manufacturer, whose conventional quarterings Lord Paulyn had not taken the trouble to efface; the vaulted roof, with its bosses and corbels in carton pierre, and gloomy as the ancient woodwork from which they had been modelled; the black and white marble floor, with skins of savage beasts laid here and there; the suits of mail glimmering in the firelight, the underling not yet having brought his taper: a dismal Udolpho-like place it looked at this hour, in spite of the chief butler's portly presence.

'A parson, I suppose,' mused the butler, when the figure of Malcolm Forde had vanished from the porch, beneath whose shadow he had lingered a few moments to look back into the house, wondering whether amidst all this pomp *she* was loved and well cared for. 'A parson, I make no doubt. What a rum lot they are, to be sure! as bad as ravens—hanging about a house where there's any one dying. One would think they went pardners with the undertaker. Let's have a look at his pasteboard,' he continued aloud, while the gas was being lighted. 'The

Reverend Malcolm Forde. Why, I'm blest if that isn't the chap she was engaged to before we married her! Fancy his coming area-sneaking here while his Ludship's out of the way.'

For about a fortnight after that evening Mr. Forde sent a messenger to Slogh-na-Dyack, at intervals of two or three days, to inquire about Lady Paulyn; and the reply being always to the effect that her ladyship was progressing favourably, he comforted himself with the idea that all danger was past, and finally told the messenger that he need go no more. His own residence at Dunallen was drawing to a close; Mr. McKenzie writing cheerily from divers Belgian towns, where he and his family were enjoying the glories and pleasures of continental travel, on an economical scale; but writing still more cheerily of his approaching return to the home-nest.

'After all, my dear Forde, there's no place like our own wee parlour; and there's nothing in the way of foreign kickshaws, partridges with stewed pears, and the Lord knows what, that I relish as much as a sheep's-head or a few broth. And I think my wife's potato-soup beats your *potage à l'Italienne* or your *purée aux pois* hollow. The hills about Spa are a poor business compared with Argyleshire; and if it wasn't for being covered with firs, would be paltry beyond comparison. And as it doesn't do for a white choker to adorn the gaming-table, I had rather a dull time of it, and was glad when we got back to Liége, where the churches and gun factories are unapproachable. I saw some wood-carving about the choir-stalls that would have set your ritualistic mouth watering, only that, now you've given yourself up to foreign missions, you've turned your back upon that kind of thing.'

Malcolm Forde's time at Dunallen was nearly ended; thank God the peril had passed! He could leave her with a heart that was almost at peace; for by this time he had schooled himself to accept his fate—the lot out of God's hand—and to pray in humility and hope for her ultimate happiness.

Thus came the last day but one of his service at Dunallen. He had been at work from early in the morning, going from dwelling to dwelling—dwellings which were chiefly of the cottage order—taking leave of people to whom he had made himself dear in the short space of his ministration among them; promising to remember them at the other end of the world, in compliance with their desire that he would sometimes think of them when he was far away. He answered them with a somewhat mournful smile, thinking of that other memory which would cleave to him for the rest of his life.

There was weeping and wailing in all these humble habitations at the prospect of his departure. Mr. McKenzie was a good man and a kind, they all protested warmly; and Mrs. McKenzie's potato-soup and honest barley-broth kept soul and body together in many a household through the bleak long winter; but Mr. McKenzie wasn't like Mr. Forde. He had a little dry way of talking to folks, and didn't enter into the very thoughts of poor bodies like his substitute. Nor could he preach so fine a sermon as Mr. Forde; a strong point with these critical Caledonians.

His day's labours were ended at last. He had trodden the heather-clad hills he loved so well for the last time; had taken his last look at Slogh-na-Dyack's white towers; and he sat by his solitary hearth thinking how very soon he should have left this well-known land to resume his work among a strange people.

Not unhopefully did he look forward to new toil, new anxieties. The eager thirst of conquest, which urges the missionary as it urges the warrior, had grown somewhat languid with him of late; he could not feel quite the old enthusiasm. 'I go to reclaim the lost among a strange people,' he thought, 'while the soul that I love best on earth may be perishing; the soul that I might have trained to such a high destiny.'

He had letters to write—much still to do before leaving Scotland; but he sat by the lonely fireside in the gloaming, lost in melancholy thought. The neat little maid-servant came to ask if she should bring the lamp; but he told her no, he liked the firelight. 'It is a pleasant light for thinking by, Meg,' he said.

A pleasant light, perhaps; but his thoughts were not pleasant. He tried to confine them to the actual business of his life, the work that lay before him in the future; but they would not be directed. They clung with a passionate regret to the scene he was about to leave. They hung around the white-walled château; they wandered in and out of those unknown chambers where Elizabeth lived; they would not be diverted from her.

'If she were well and happy it would be different,' he said to himself, in self-exculpation.

He sat on till the chapel clock had struck nine. The October night was blusterous, wild gusts rattling the window-frames, and rustling the ivy with a gruesome and ghostly sound, as of disembodied souls striving for admittance. The moon was up, and by fits and starts emerged from a stormy sea of blackest clouds, lighting up the wild landscape, the water at the foot of the hill. It was during one of these sudden bursts of moonlight that Mr. Forde, happening suddenly to look up, saw a strange figure outside his window; a face white as the moonlight, peering in at him through the glass. For a moment he looked at it in dumb wonder, taking it for the embodiment of his own troubled fancies, a mere visionary creature; as if that melancholy sound of the ivy leaves against the glass had made itself a shape out of the shadows.

It was very real, however. A hand tapped upon the pane, with a hurried imperious tapping. He got up from his chair, and went over to the window.

Great Heaven! it was that one woman whose image absorbed his every thought; it was Elizabeth!

'Let me in!' she cried piteously, in tones that seemed strange to him; stranger even than her presence in that spot. He opened the window softly.

'I will come round to the door and let you in,' he said; 'for Heaven's sake what has happened?'

'Only that I have cheated them all at last,' she said, looking at him with wild beseeching eyes; 'I have broken loose from my bondage. O Malcolm, you will not let them take me back again?'

Something — an unutterable indefinable something—in her tones and looks struck him with a sharper pain than he had felt even yet; though almost all his thoughts of her had been pain. He rushed across the room, and the tiny hall beyond it, to the door, only a few paces from the window by which she stood. He opened it quickly, went out into the wintry night, and found her still rapping impatiently upon the pane, as if she had not heard or comprehended what he said to her.

She was clad in some loose long garment of the dressing-gown species, and had a shawl flung carelessly over her shoulders; but neither hat nor bonnet. Her long rippling hair fell loosely about her, mixed with the folds of her shawl.

'Dear Lady Paulyn,' he said very gently, 'what could have induced you to come here at such an hour? Good heavens! you have surely not walked?' he added hastily; looking down the long moonlit road, where there was no vestige of any vehicle.

'Yes; I have come all the way on foot, and alone. I was afraid at first that I might not find you; but there was some instinct led me right, I think. Sometimes I saw you a little way before me in the moonlight, and you turned, now and then, and smiled and beckoned to me. Your smile drew me after you. Why do you live so far off, Malcolm? you were so much nearer at Hawleigh. I remember that morning I came to see you, only to find you gone—it seemed so short a walk; but to-night it was like walking on for ever and ever.'

'Come into the house,' he said, in a curious half-muffled voice, a deadly fear rending his heart. 'Come into the warm room, Elizabeth; you are shivering.'

'Not with cold,' she said hastily; 'with fear.'

'Fear! of what?'

'That they'll follow me, and take me away from you. They'll guess where I've come, you know; as you and I are engaged to be married. My horrible jailers will hunt me down, Malcolm; Hilda at their head. Hilda, who is the worst of all—not rough and cruel with her hands like the others—but cruel with her cold watchful eyes, that are looking me into my grave.'

What was this? the delirium of fever? He had been told that the fever had passed, that she was almost well. They had deceived him evidently; they denied his right to know what progress she made towards recovery or towards death. They had mocked him with their lying messages.

He put her shawl round her, and drew her into the house. He could keep her here long enough for her to rest and refresh herself, while a messenger went to Slogh-na-Dyack to fetch a carriage to convey her home. This was obviously his duty. She had talked wildly of her jailers; she had entreated him not to deliver her up to them; yet his first act must needs be in a manner to betray her. His duty was clearly to restore her into the hands of her friends.

That wild horror of Hilda and of her nurses could but be the raving of delirium. They were doubtless kind enough in their way—even if it were not the kindest way—only hired service, or the task-work imposed by duty. It was common for these poor fever-distracted souls to exhibit a horror of their best friends—to fly from them even as she had fled. No, there was nothing for him to do but to restore her to her own home—to that lonely pile which had seemed to him so darksome and gloomy a habitation that autumn twilight when he crossed its threshold for the first time.

He led her into the parlour, where pine-logs and sea-coal were burning cheerily, led her into the ruddy home-like light, her weary head resting on his shoulder: as it had never rested since the night when he asked her to be his wife, and let all the scheme of his existence drift away from him upon the floodtide of passion. He placed her in the big easy-chair by the hearth, removed her shawl, damp with the night dew, and then planted himself by the opposite side of the mantelpiece, watching her with grave anxiety, thinking even in this sad moment how fair a picture she made in the firelight, a sad forlorn face with troubled eyes, a listless figure half-shrouded in a veil of golden-brown hair. If it were his duty, as he felt it was, to communicate with her friends, there was time enough to dispatch his messenger. He wanted her to speak a little more clearly first, to discover the full significance of her fear.

She sat for some minutes in silence staring absently at the fire, with a half smile upon her face, as if exhausted by her long walk, and feeling a physical satisfaction in mere warmth and rest. Then, after what seemed to Malcolm a very long pause, she looked slowly round the room, still smiling, and this time with more meaning in her smile.

'How pretty your room looks in the firelight!' she said in her old light tone, which smote him to the heart at such a time. 'But your rooms are always pretty, with books and things—much prettier than my grand rooms, crowded with pictures and gilding and finery, and a hundred colours that make my eyes ache to look at them. I like this sober brown-looking parlour, like an interior by Rembrandt. This is the first time that I have been in any room of yours since I came to you that morning at Hawleigh. But we were not engaged to be married in those days!' she added, smiling innocently up at him, as if she were saying the most reasonable, the most natural thing in this world.

'Our engagement!' he said gravely, 'that is an auld sang, and came to an end long ago. Let us talk of the future, Lady Paulyn, not of the past.'

She watched him as he spoke, with a curious look, as if she saw him talking without hearing what he said.

'It was before we were engaged,' she went on, pursuing her own line of thought. 'How soon are we to be married, Malcolm? When we are married you can take me away from that dreadful room,' with a shudder, 'that horrid room where I lie awake night after night watching the candle burn slowly down—O, how slowly it burns!—and the reflection of the flame in the shining oak-panel. It was clever of me to find out that about the candle, wasn't it? They took away my watch, and got tired of telling me what o'clock it was, or were too unkind to do it; and then I thought of King Alfred and the candles, and knew by their burning when morning had ne[ar] come.'

He sighed—a heartbroken sigh—and sat down [by] her, taking her hand gently. 'Dear Lady Paulyn,' [he] began, with a stress upon the name, 'I want to [de]cide, with your help, what we had better do. T[his] long dreary walk must have tired you so much. Y[ou] have been very ill—'

She turned upon him sharply, with flashing e[yes.] 'Do not say that to me,' she cried angrily; 'tha[t's] what all the doctors said: "Dear lady, you have b[een] very ill;" talking to me in their soothing sugary to[nes] as if they were reasoning with a baby in arms. I t[old] them that I was not ill—that I was quite as well [as I] had ever been in my life—only that I wanted to [be] let out of that hideous room, to go out upon the hi[lls,] to come to you, Malcolm,' with sudden tendernes[s.]

'And you see I was right,' she went on, afte[r a] little pause. 'If I were ill, do you suppose I co[uld] have walked ever so many miles? and I came al[ong] almost as fast as the wind. I ran part of the w[ay.] Could I do that if I were ill, Malcolm?'

He was silent for a few moments, his head tur[ned] away from her and from the firelight, his face q[uite] hidden. The first sound that broke that silence [was] a smothered sob.

She looked at him wonderingly.

'Malcolm, why are you unhappy about me? Don't you understand that I am not ill? What does it matter to us if all those doctors talk nonsense? You can send them all away when we are married.'

'Elizabeth,' he said with tender earnestness, taking her thin cold hand in his, and holding it while he spoke,—alas, there was no sign of bodily fever in that poor little hand! it was that greater fever of the mind which he perceived here, with supreme anguish, —'Elizabeth, there is a kind of illness in which the mind is the chief sufferer, an illness of which it seems to me the best means of cure are in the hands of the patient, and not the doctor. Patience and resignation, dear, are the means of cure which God has given to us all. If anything has made you unhappy, if anything has disturbed your peace of mind, pray to Him for help, for consolation, for cure. They will come, Elizabeth; believe me, they will come.'

She looked at him wonderingly for a few minutes, as if there were something in his words that made her thoughtful. He was the first person who had ever spoken to her of her mind, who had ever boldly told her that all was not well there. The doctors had simpered at her, and tut-tuted and patted her gently on the head, as if she had suddenly gone backward in years and become a child of two. They had made pretty little affectionate speeches of a sugar-plum fashion, never giving her a direct answer to her eager questions, putting off everything blandly till to-morrow, till she began to think the order of the universe was changed, and time was all to-morrow. And then they left her to lie on her bed and wonder from dawn to sunset, from night till morning, and to weave strange romances in her ever-working brain, for lack of any reality in her life except the horrible reality of the room she hated and the nurses who ill-used her. But this was part-and-parcel of the magical process of isolation whereby she was to recover her wits.

'There is nothing the matter with my mind,' she said. 'What should there be the matter now that I am with you, and happy? There never was anything the matter with me except the silent horror of that room, and those rough-handed women who stared at me, and worried me from morning till night with medicines and messes, jellies and beefteas and things, making believe that I was ill. But you won't give me back to them—you won't let them take me away from you? Promise me that, Malcolm; mind, you must promise me that,' half rising from her chair and clinging to him.

'My dearest, do not ask me to make an impossible

promise. I have no alternative. It is my duty to restore you to your friends. You cannot remain here; and where can you so properly be as in your own house? Try to think, Elizabeth, what the world would say if it knew that you wished to leave your husband and your own proper home!'

'My husband!' she repeated, with a cold laugh—'my husband! That is what Hilda said to me one day. The nurses talk of *my* delusions; why, there can be no delusion so wild as that! As if I could have any other husband than you, Malcolm, after that night in the vicarage garden when I almost asked you to marry me. My husband! Go back to my husband, go away from *you* to my husband! What, Malcolm, are you going to talk nonsense like all the rest?' she asked, looking round her with a helpless bewildered air. 'I begin to think that every one in the world is going mad except myself.'

'Elizabeth, if you would only try to remember. It is quite true that old promise was made, dear, and you and I were to be together all our lives. But Providence has ruled otherwise. A foolish mistake of mine divided us, and then, after a little while, you found another lover whose constancy and devotion must have gained your gratitude and esteem, if not your love, for you married him. Remember, Elizabeth, you are the wife of Lord Paulyn. You owe affection, duty, obedience, to him, and you are bound to go back to the shelter of his roof. If it seems dismal and strange to you while you are so ill, dear, be assured that fancy will pass away. Only pray for God's help, pray to Him to banish all evil fancies.'

'Evil fancies!' she cried, staring at him with wide-open wondering eyes, and an expression that was half perplexity, half contempt for his persistent folly. 'You are like the rest, Malcolm, mad, mad! How dare you say that I am married! how dare you say that I have ever been false to you! Good heavens, have I not thought of you without ceasing since the first night of our engagement, that night when we stood by the vicarage gate, Malcolm, and you confessed you loved me? I did wring that confession from you at last; and O, how proud it made me, as if I had tamed a lion and made him lie down at my feet!'

She was silent for a few moments, looking down at the fire with a happy smile, placidly happy in that supreme egotism, that curious self-concentration, which is one of the characteristics of lunacy, as if living over again that hour of triumphant love, the hour in which she had proved that passion may be stronger than principle even in a good man's breast.

'Why do you talk to me of husbands!' she cried,

with a little burst of anger. 'There is a man at Slogh-na-Dyack who ill-treated me, hurt me with his strong cruel grasp, dragged me away from the window when I wanted to escape to you. He is not my husband. You won't send me back to *him*, will you, Malcolm? O God, you could not be so cruel as that! If you knew how I watched day after day, night after night, before this chance came, before I could get away from that hateful room! They kept my door locked in my own house—think of that, Malcolm— the door locked upon me as if I had been a refractory child! I watched them to find out where they put the keys of the two doors. But they would not let me see, and it was only to-night for the first time that I cheated them. They were both out of the room—no one there, not even Hilda, my arch enemy, who has tried to poison me. Yes, Malcolm, you will not believe, but I have seen it in her face—only I have refused to eat, and baffled her that way. I have refused to touch anything for days, till they forced me to swallow their abominable messes,' with a look of unutterable disgust, 'bending over me with their odious breath, and clutching me with their great hot hands. Malcolm!' starting up from her chair, and appealing to him passionately, with outstretched hands, 'swear that you will not give me back into 'their power! Kill me if you like, if you have quite left off loving me, if I am no use to the world or you —kill me, Malcolm; death from your hands would not be painful—but don't send me back to that locked room! Good heavens, why do you stand there looking at me like that? Are you afraid of them, afraid of Hilda Disney, afraid of that stony cruel man you call my husband?'

'What am I to do?' he cried, not yet able to master even his own thoughts, at sea on a stormy ocean of doubt and pity and love and honour. To see her thus, beautiful even in the utter wreck of reason, loving, humble, confiding, the pride that had been her blemish extinguished for ever—to see her thus, casting herself upon his love, appealing to his manhood, and yet to feel himself powerless to help her in the smallest degree, unable to stand for a moment between her and her sorrow—this was an ordeal beyond the worst peril of his wanderings, beyond the circle of yelping savages, the fire kindled at his feet, which he had considered among the possibilities of his career. He constrained himself by a supreme effort of his troubled mind to contemplate the situation calmly, as if he had been interested only in his priestly character, called upon to advise or direct in such an emergency.

'No,' he exclaimed at last; 'you shall not go back to Slogh-na-Dyack, if I can prevent it.'

She gave a cry of joy, a wild passionate cry, as of a soul released from purgatory.

'Thank God!' she cried. 'O, I knew that you would not send me back! Let me stay with you, Malcolm; let me follow you in all your wanderings. Do you think I fear hardship, or famine, or weariness, where you are? Let me teach the little children in those savage lands. Children have always loved me, and I them. Remember how I nursed the children at Hawleigh. Let me go with you, Malcolm. I will be anything you order me to be, a slave to work for those wretched people,' with a faint shudder, as if she had not yet overcome her idea of the general commonness of the missionary order. 'I will endure everything—toil, danger, death—if you will let me be with you.'

He did not answer her, except with a long look of sorrowful tenderness—parting the loose hair gently from her forehead with a protecting touch, which was curiously different from the patronising pattings of the faculty—contemplating her with a deploring tenderness. He could not answer her. To reason—to attempt to awaken dormant memories—seemed useless. The doors of her brain had shut up the story of her wedded life. It was not in his power to recall her to a sense of her actual position—to rend the veil which shut out the realities—leaving her soul in a fool's paradise of dreams.

He had arranged his plan of action meanwhile. He rang for the lamp, and the honest Scottish lassie, entering with the lighted moderator, beheld with obvious consternation the figure of a lady, with pale face and disordered hair, clad in a long purple garment, slashed and faced with satin—a garment such as Maggie the housemaid had never looked upon before, a garment fastened with cords and tassels, which the lady's restless fingers knotted and unknotted again and again while Maggie stared at her.

'Tell your brother to saddle Trim,' said Mr. Forde, in his quietest manner; 'I want a message taken to the railway station at Ellensbridge.'

He looked at his watch thoughtfully. No, it would hardly be too late to send a telegram from that small station.

'Ye'll no' be sending the night, Mr. Forde,' said the girl, 'the station'll be shut.'

'No, it won't, Maggie. Tell your brother to get the pony ready this minute. And then come back to me for the message.'

He took the lamp to a desk on the other side

of the room, where he had the blank forms for telegrams and all business appliances, and, without farther deliberation, wrote the following message:

'*Malcolm Forde, Dunallen, Argyleshire, to Gertrude Luttrell, Hawleigh, Devon, England.*

'Your sister, Lady Paulyn, is dangerously ill. Come at once to this place. A case of urgent necessity. Telegraph reply.'

He filled another form with almost the same words addressed to Mrs. Chevenix, Eaton-place-south. And having delivered these to Maggie, with strict instructions as to haste and care in the manner of transmitting them, he began to consider how soon either of these women could reach that remote spot. It was too late for Mrs. Chevenix to leave town by the limited mail. She could only arrive at Dunallen upon the following night, just twenty-four hours after the sending of the telegram. And during that interval how was he to protect Elizabeth from her natural protectors—from people who had an unassailable right to the custody of this helpless creature?

His only hope lay in the chance that they might not guess where she had gone; yet he hardly dared hope as much as that, when Miss Disney knew that he was in the neighbourhood, and doubtless knew that he had once been Elizabeth's betrothed husband. His first thought, the telegrams being dispatched, was to find her a fitting refuge. He had friends enough in the cosy little hill-side colony, friends who, in the common acceptation of the phrase, would have gone through fire and water to serve him, though they had only known him seven weeks. He debated for a little while—a very little while—for moments were precious, and he had already lost much time, and then decided upon his plan of action. Two ancient maiden ladies, his devoted admirers, lived in a snug little villa hardly five minutes' walk from the manse—friendly Scotch bodies, upon whose kindness and singleness of heart he could rely. With these two ladies he might find the fittest shelter for the forlorn being who had cast herself upon his care. Lodged safely here, she might, perhaps, escape pursuit for a little while —just long enough to bring the friends of her girlhood round her, so that she might at least have her sister by her side when she went back to Slogh-na-Dyack.

'Wrap your shawl closely round you, Lady Paulyn,' he said. 'I am going to take you to a house where you can sleep to-night—to friends who will take care of you.'

'Friends!' she cried; 'I have no friends in the world but you. Let me stay here—with you. O, Malcolm, you are not going to send me away after all?'

'I am not going to send you back to the people you fear—as I believe without reason. I am going to put you in the charge of two good friends of mine—kind old Scotch women, who will be very good to you.'

'I want no one's goodness,' she exclaimed impatiently. 'Why can I not stay here with you?'

'It is quite impossible.'

'But why?'

'Because you have a husband and a house of your own.'

She shook her head angrily. 'He is madder than the rest,' she muttered.

'And I should do very wrong to detain you here. I fear that, if I did my duty, I should at once communicate with your household at Sloghna-Dyack.'

'You will not do that!' she cried, starting up, and clinging to his arm.

'No, Elizabeth, I cannot do that—against your

wish. I will see you placed in safe hands, and perhaps to-morrow one of your sisters, or your aunt, may be here to protect you.'

'One of my sisters,' she repeated dreamily. 'I should like to have Blanche with me. I was always fond of Blanche.'

'Come, then. The less time we lose the better.'

He went out into the hall, she following him, and thence to the garden in front of the manse. He gave her his arm as they went out into the windy road, white in the moonlight, but they had scarcely crossed the boundary when she gave a shrill scream and darted back towards the house. Two women, one tall and gaunt-looking, were standing in the road, a few paces from a brougham, which seemed to be waiting for them.

The tall woman advanced to meet Mr. Forde, the other ran back to the carriage, and exclaimed to some one inside, 'We've found her, Miss Disney, we've found her!'

'What do you want?' asked Malcolm, his heart sinking with a sickness as of death itself. Vain had been his hope of putting himself between her and the people to whom she belonged.

'That lady,' said the female grenadier, pointing to Elizabeth, who stood in the porch watching them,

'Lady Paulyn. It was Miss Disney told us to come here to look for her.'

'Yes,' said Hilda, who had alighted from the brougham; 'and if you had been honest enough to tell me of Lady Paulyn's escape at the time it occurred, instead of three hours afterwards, I should have been here ever so long ago. I daresay you remember me, Mr. Forde,' she added, turning to Malcolm. 'I met you at luncheon one day at Hawleigh Vicarage. My name is Disney. I am Lord Paulyn's cousin.'

'I remember you perfectly, Miss Disney.'

'I am sorry we should meet again under such lamentable circumstances. You have of course perceived poor Lady Paulyn's sad condition? Has she been here long?'

'A little more than an hour, I should think. What made you suppose that she would come here?'

Hilda hesitated a little before replying.

'Because you are about the only person she knows in this neighbourhood.'

'An isolated position for any woman to occupy,' said Malcolm, 'and I should imagine eminently calculated to depress the spirits or even to unsettle the mind.'

'Lady Paulyn had my society and her husband's,

sir; and I do not believe solitude has had anything to do with the melancholy state of her mind.'

'She has a strange aversion to returning to Sloghna-Dyack,' said Mr. Forde, 'and a horror of her nurses, perhaps a natural feeling in her delirious state. Now I have friends here; two simple-minded kindly old ladies who would be very glad to take charge of her for a few days. You might remain with her, if you pleased; and you could by that means withdraw her from a place about which she has such an unhappy feeling.'

He did not want to give her up to them without a struggle, yet reason told him any struggle would be useless. Miss Disney's inflexible face, looking at him sternly in the moonlight, was not the face of a woman to be turned from her own set purpose by an appeal that might be made to her compassion.

'I could not possibly sanction such an extraordinary proceeding,' she said. 'Lord Paulyn is away from home, and in his absence I feel myself responsible for his wife's safety. I cannot forgive the nurses for their shameful neglect this evening.'

'There's no being up to the artfulness of 'em,' said the tall nurse. 'This evening was the first time the key of that door was ever out of my own keeping, owing to my having torn my pocket, and not liking to trust to it, and put that blessed key in a little chiny jar on the mantelpiece.'

'Will you ask my cousin to come to the carriage, Mr. Forde?' said Miss Disney with a business-like air; 'we need not lose any more time.'

'You had better come into the house for a little while and talk to her quietly. There is no occasion to let her feel she is taken back like a prisoner.'

Hilda complied rather unwillingly, and Mr. Forde led the way to the porch, where Elizabeth stood waiting the issue of events.

'You are not going to give me up, are you?' she asked.

'I have no power to detain you.'

'Then you are a coward!' she cried passionately. 'Is this what men have come to since the age of chivalry, when a man would leap among lions to pick up a woman's glove? *You* go among the heathen; *you* brave the rage of savages, their tortures, their poisoned arrows, their flames! Why, all that they say you have done can be nothing but lies, when you are afraid to oppose her,' pointing contemptuously to Miss Disney.

'Elizabeth,' he said earnestly, trying to pierce the confusion of her mind, 'there are social laws stronger than fire or sword, and the law that gives a woman to her husband is the strongest of them all, for it is a divine law as well as a social one. I dare not come between you and those who have the best right to protect you. But I can interfere to redress your wrongs if they are false to their trust. I do not stand by unconcerned in this matter. Wherever you are, at Slogh-na-Dyack as well as in this house, I shall be interested in your welfare; at hand to give you all the help I can give, counsel and consolation as a minister of God's word, or advice as a man of the world. I have telegraphed to your sisters and your aunt, and I feel little doubt they will be with you to-morrow night.'

'A most uncalled-for interference,' said Hilda disdainfully. 'The doctors have forbidden any intercourse between Lady Paulyn and her relations.'

'What, do the doctors choose the time when she has most need of familiar friends and old associations to cut her off from them altogether? Wise doctors, Miss Disney! Common sense and natural affection suggest a better system of cure for a mind ill at ease.'

'You may pretend to know more than scientific men who have made this malady the study of their lives,' replied Hilda; 'but however that may be, I can only tell you that should the Miss Luttrells be so foolish as to come to Lord Paulyn's house uninvited by him, they will not be allowed to see their sister.'

'We will see about that when they are here.'

Elizabeth stood between them silently. A vacant look had stolen over the pale melancholy face. She uttered no farther remonstrance, no farther upbraiding, but went with Hilda unresistingly, apathetic, or half unconscious where she was being taken. The fitful flame had died out into darkness. She was a creature without a mind; submissive, indifferent; to awaken by and by to a sense of her imprisonment and to vain anger and fury, like a wild animal that has been netted while it slept.

CHAPTER XI.

*'No joy from favourable fortune
Can overweigh the anguish of this stroke.'*

THE night that followed was the darkest Malcolm Forde had ever known till now, darker even than that which followed Alice Fraser's death; for are not the dead that are already dead better than the living that are yet alive? And to the believer death has no positive horror; it is only the anguish of separation; a human sorrow; a human longing; a sharp pain, tempered always by that divine hope which makes this earthly life verily a pilgrimage leading to fair worlds beyond it.

But this death in life called madness—this living death, which may endure for the length of the longest life—is more bitter than the coffin and the grave. To know her miserable and helpless in the hands of people she feared—linked to a husband she had never even pretended to love—was to know her in a state as much worse than death as waking agony is worse than dreamless sleep. Never until this hour, when he looked round his empty room, the vacant chair where she had sat, the expiring fire into which those lovely eyes had gazed with their far-off dreaming look—never until now had he fully realised how he loved her; how little the life he had lived and the work he had done in five long years had served to divide him from her; how near and dear she was to him still.

Sleep, or even the semblance of rest, the miserable pretence of going to bed, was impossible to him that night. He walked down to Slogh-na-Dyack, down to the little bay where the troubled waters broke against the shore with a dismal moaning, where the reflection of the moon was blotted out every now and then by black wind-driven clouds. It was a dreary night, bleak and wintry; not a favourable season for midnight wanderings, or patient vigil beneath the window of a beloved sleeper; yet Malcolm Forde paced the narrow strip of beach below Lord Paulyn's garden, a strip that was covered at high tide, until the morning gray. That patient watch might be useless—was useless no doubt—but it was all that he could do; the sole service he could render to the woman he loved. He saw the lighted windows on the chief upper floor—lights that never waned through the weary night—and he felt very sure they belonged to the rooms inhabited by Elizabeth. Had a cry of anguish broken from those dear lips, it must have pierced the stillness of the night when the wind was low, and reached him on his beat. Sometimes, when the shrill blast shrieked in the mountain gorge upon the opposite shore, he almost fancied the sound of human anguish was mixed with the voice of the wind. It was a sad unsatisfactory vigil; but it was better to be there, beneath her windows, than to be lying sleepless miles away, beyond reach of her loudest cry. When day came, and the first gray threads of smoke crept up from the Gothic chimneys, he went round to the chief entrance, rang the bell, and inquired of the sleepy housemaid who answered it if Lady Paulyn had passed a quiet night.

'Ask the head nurse,' he said, as the girl stared at him vaguely, 'and then come back and tell me exactly what she says,' emphasising his request with a donation.

The girl departed, and returned quickly enough.

'Much the same as usual, sir, Nurse Barber says, and would you please leave your name?'

'Give that to Miss Disney,' he said, handing the girl his card, on which he had written the date, and 7 A.M. He wanted Hilda to know that he was vigilant, and was not to be deterred from watchfulness by any fear of slander or of Lord Paulyn's displeasure.

This done, he went back to Dunallen, went back to the early service in the chapel, and to another day's work in the quiet little parish where he had made himself beloved. There was nothing more for him to do, he thought, than to wait till the arrival of the fast train from the South, which would not reach the station at Ellensbridge till half-past nine o'clock at night, even if it were punctual; an event not always to be counted as a certainty on a Scotch railway.

He found two telegrams on his study-table when he went back to the manse after his morning's work. The first from Gertrude, 'I leave Hawleigh at 9 A.M. to-day, Thursday, and shall leave London for Ellensbridge by the limited mail.' The second, a vague and helpless message from Mrs. Chevenix, entreating for detailed information, and pleading indifferent health as a reason for not coming to Scotland, if such a journey might possibly be avoided. Mrs. Chevenix had squandered three-and-sixpence worth of telegraphic communication in the endeavour to represent herself ardently desirous of flying to her beloved niece's sick-bed, yet unhappily obliged to remain in Eaton-place-south.

Not till to-morrow therefore could Elizabeth's sad

eyes be gladdened by the sight of a familiar face, not till to-morrow could sisterly arms enfold that poor sufferer. For many hours to come Malcolm Forde must be content to leave her to the tender mercy of hired nurses and Hilda Disney. He could do nothing for her except pray, and all his thoughts in this bitter time were prayers for her.

The railway to Ellensbridge was only a loop line, and that stern adherence to the hours set down in time-tables which is demanded by southern passengers on main lines was here unknown. If a train came in an hour or so after time, no one wondered. Railway officials placidly remarked that 'she was joost a wee bittie late the dee,' and that was all. Passengers herded meekly together on the narrow platform and gazed up and down the line, and saw other trains arrive and depart—trains that seemed to have no place in the time-table—or watched the leisurely shunting of a string of coal-trucks, and made no murmur. The marvel would have been if a train at Ellensbridge had ever come up to time.

Mr. Forde paced the platform with infinite impatience when the hour had gone by at which the train with passengers from the South should have arrived, waiting for the signal that should announce Gertrude Luttrell's coming. There was nothing doing at the station just at this time; even the string of empty coal-trucks stood idle, an unemployed engine on a siding puffed and snorted lazily, while the stoker off duty amused himself with the gymnastics of a disreputable-looking monkey. The day was wet and depressing; that fine straight rain, which to the impatient tourist appears sometimes to be the normal atmosphere of Scotland, filled the air; the kind of day in which Cockney travellers in the Trosachs stare hopelessly at Benvenue, looming big through the gray mist, and think they might almost as well be looking at the dome of St. Paul's from Blackfriars Bridge.

The train came slowly in at last, serenely unconscious of being three-quarters of an hour behind time, a diminutive train of two carriages and an engine; and out of one of the carriages Gertrude Luttrell looked with a pale anxious face, a face which sent a thrill of pain through the heart of Malcolm Forde, for it seemed to him that in this wan and faded countenance he saw a likeness of that altered beauty he had looked upon a little while ago.

'What is the matter with my sister?' she asked nervously, directly she was on the platform. 'O, Mr. Forde, am I too late? Is—'

She stopped, and burst into tears. He led her into the little waiting-room, and reassured her there was no immediate danger.

'Thank God!' she cried, with a strange fervour. 'O, Mr. Forde, it seems like a dream, seeing you here in this strange place; it seems like a dream to be here myself. I came without loss of an hour; I couldn't do any more than that, could I? Elizabeth has not been a good sister to me, or indeed to any of us. Her prosperity has made very little difference to us; we went on living our old dull life just the same after her marriage, and she did hardly anything to brighten it. Even long ago, before you came to Hawleigh, she was always cold and unloving towards me, sneered at my humble efforts to do right, set herself up against me in the strength of her beauty.'

'It is hardly a time for complaints of this kind,' said Mr. Forde, with grave displeasure. 'Your sister is in great trouble.'

'Have I not come? Am I not here to be with her? O, why are you always so hard upon me, Mr. Forde? Just the same after all these years. I would do anything in the world for her. It is not my fault if her married life is unhappy.'

'Do not let us waste time in purposeless talk. I

have a carriage ready to take you to your sister's house. I will tell you everything on the way.'

In the carriage he told her the real nature of her sister's illness, the ruin that had befallen that bright reckless mind; told her his hope of speedy cure in a case where there was no hereditary taint, no shattered constitution, only the fever and confusion of a mind ill at ease, a soul seeking peace where there was no peace. He told her of his confidence in the happy influence of a familiar presence, of old associations, sisterly affection.

Gertrude was inexpressibly shocked; a curious stillness crept over her; she left off making vague attempts to explain her own conduct in relation to her sister, which had never been called into question by Mr. Forde; ceased to make little sidelong attacks upon Elizabeth; but became mute, with the aspect of one upon whom a heavy blow has fallen. Only when they were near Slogh-na-Dyack did she speak.

'Can you say with confidence that you believe she will recover?' she asked; 'that you do not think she will be—mad—all her life?'

'I can say nothing of the kind,' he answered sadly. 'I can only say that I try to put my trust in God throughout this trial, as in others that have gone before it. But this seems harder than the rest.'

They were at Slogh-na-Dyack by this time; but here bitter disappointment, a disappointment near akin to despair, awaited them, for upon Gertrude announcing herself as Lady Paulyn's sister, and requesting to be taken straight to the invalid's apartments, a vacant-looking flat-faced footman informed her that her ladyship had left Slogh-na-Dyack for the South just four-and-twenty hours ago.

'What!' cried Mr. Forde, who was standing on the threshold of the door, while Gertrude stood a little way within, staring helplessly at the blank face of the footman. 'Do you mean to tell me that Lady Paulyn was allowed to travel in her state of health?'

'Yes, sir. The London doctor and one of the nurses went with her.'

'They went with her, but where?'

'To London, I believe, sir. As far as I could make out from what was said.'

'Where is Miss Disney? Let me see Miss Disney.'

'Miss Disney have left also, sir.'

'Then let me see some one who can tell me what all this means. This lady is your mistress's sister, who has travelled five hundred miles to see her, only to be told that she is gone, no one knows where. Is there any one else in the house who can explain this business?'

The footman shook his head despondently.

'There's Colter the butler, sir,' he said; '*he* might know something, and there's my lady's own maid.'

'Let me see her,' exclaimed Mr. Forde; whereupon the footman, always with a despondent air, ushered them into the library, a darksome but splendid apartment, which the Glasgow manufacturer had furnished with antique carved shelves for books that had never been supplied, a room in which literature was represented by a waste-paper basket, a what-not crammed with stale newspapers, a *Ruff's Guide*, *Post and Paddock*, and three or four numbers of *Baily's Magazine*.

Here Malcolm Forde paced to and fro, his soul shaken to its lowest deep, while Gertrude sat in a huge arm-chair and cried feebly. What had they done with Elizabeth? What sinister motive had they in this sudden flight? What had they done with the helpless creature who had come to him for refuge, casting herself upon his pity, entreating with heart-piercing accents for shelter and protection? And he had refused to shelter her. The fear of injuring her in the sight of the world, or of widening the breach between her and her husband, had been stronger with him than love and pity; the anxious desire to do his duty had triumphed over the voice of his heart, which had said, 'Claim a brother's right to protect her in her affliction, and defy the world.'

He had done that which he had deemed the only thing possible for him to do. He had summoned her nearest of kin, the sister who had a right to be by her side at such a time, even in defiance of a husband. He had done this, and behold! it was as if he had done nothing for her. Where had they taken her— on what dismal journey had she gone—with a nurse and a doctor? His heart sank as he brooded upon that question. There was only one answer that presented itself—an answer that was horrible to think of.

The door was opened after some delay by Mr. Colter, the butler, who had been enjoying the morning in a dressing-gown-and-slipper condition, loitering over a late breakfast and making the most of the family's absence, and had just made a hasty toilet in order to come to the front and see what was meant by Miss Luttrell's unlooked-for appearance on the scene. Behind him came a young woman with a nervous air, and eyelids that were reddened with weeping.

'This young person is Lady Paulyn's maid, Sarah

Todd,' said the butler blandly. 'I have sent for her to see you, sir, as I was informed you had expressed a wish to that effeck. But there is no information she can give you about my lady as I don't know as well as her. I'm sorry you should have made such a long journey for nothink, ma'am,' he added, turning to Miss Luttrell, 'but if you'd wrote, or telegraphed, the trouble might have been avided.'

'I want to know all about this business, sir,' said Malcolm Forde with his sternest air. 'At whose bidding and in whose custody was Lady Paulyn removed from this house?'

'By the horder of her medical adviser, sir, and under his protection, with a nurse halso in attendance upon her.'

'Indeed! Then Lord Paulyn was not with his wife?'

'No, sir. My lord is in Invernesshire.'

'What! Then it was in his absence Lady Paulyn was removed?'

'Certingly, sir—which the removal of her ladyship had been arranged before his lordship left this house. It was his lordship's wish to be away at the time— with a natural delickisy of feeling.'

'Where has Lady Paulyn been taken? To her house in Park-lane?'

'No, sir.'

Here Sarah Todd, the maid, dissolved into tears; at which the butler stared sternly at her, informing her that the lady and gentleman wanted none of her snivelling.

'Pray do not scold her,' said Mr. Forde. 'I am glad to see that she can feel for her mistress. And now perhaps you will be good enough to tell me where Lady Paulyn has been taken—if not to her town house?'

'That, sir, is a question which I do not feel myself at liberty to hanswer.'

'You need not stand upon punctilio. You can waive the natural delicacy of mind which you no doubt share with your master. I can guess the worst you can tell me. Lady Paulyn has been taken to a private madhouse.'

'I believe, sir, it is somethink in the way of an asylum. Strictly private, of course, and everythink upon the footing of a gentleman's 'ouse,' replied the butler, softening, with a view to a possible donation, slipped unobtrusively into his palm presently, when he was escorting these visitors back to their carriage.

'Can you give me the exact address of the house?'

'No, sir. Everthink was kep extraordinary close. I heard it was somewheres near London. Even the nurse didn't know where she was gone.'

'One of the nurses went with Lady Paulyn, you say? Which was she—the tall woman?'

'Yes, sir.'

'And what became of the other?'

'She left by the same train, sir, to go back to her own home.'

'Do you know *her* address?'

'No, sir.'

'Nor you?' turning to the maid.

'No, sir. But she came from an institution somewhere near the Strand. You might hear of her perhaps there.'

'Will you oblige me by writing down the names of both nurses on a slip of paper?' said Mr. Forde.

There were an inkstand and portfolio on the table, and the girl sat down immediately and wrote two names in a neat school-girl hand.

'"Mrs. Barber," that's the tall nurse who went with Lady Paulyn, sir. "Mrs. Gurbage," that's the one who went home.'

'Thanks. I must try to find Mrs. Gurbage. And now tell this lady all you can. I'll leave you with her for a few minutes while I talk to Mr. Colter in the hall. Tell her how Lady Paulyn was when she left this place.'

The girl shook her head sorrowfully. 'There's very little I can tell, sir, though I loved my lady dearly, for she was always a dear good mistress to me. A little hasty sometimes, but O, so generous and kind. But from the time she began to be so ill they wouldn't let me go near her, though I know she used to ask for me, for I've stood outside her door sometimes for half-an-hour at a time and listened and heard her call me, and then cry so pitifully, "Let me have some one with me that I know—for God's sake send me some one I know!"'

The girl remained with Miss Luttrell, while Mr. Forde and the butler went out into the hall and waited for them. But there was little more to be extracted either from man or maid.

They only knew that after the fever Lady Paulyn had gone out of her mind. She had suffered an attack of the same kind after her baby's death—only not so severe an attack. The doctors had come backwards and forwards, and it had ended by her ladyship being removed under the care of one of them—whose very name the butler had never heard.

'Everythink was kep so close,' he repeated; 'and

it would have been as much as our places were worth to show any curossity.'

Thus, after a little while, they left Slogh-na-Dyack in darkest ignorance, and Mr. Forde took Miss Luttrell to the manse, to give her rest and refreshment before their next move, which must be to London.

The woman he loved better than all things else in this lower world was hidden away from him in a madhouse. Hard trial of his faith, who had made duty his rule of life. If he had followed the dictates of his heart that night, he might have found her some safe refuge—might have saved her from this living grave. With a bitter pang he recalled that last contemptuous look which she had flung him when she accused him of cowardice.

CHAPTER XII.

'That was my true love's voice. Where is he? I heard him call. I am free! Nobody shall hinder me. I will fly to his neck, and lie on his bosom. He called Margaret! He stood upon the threshold. In the midst—through the howling and chattering of hell—through the grim, devilish scoffing—I knew the sweet, the loving tone again.'

A SPACIOUS old-fashioned mansion north of London, among the green byroads between Barnet and Watford; a noble old house, red brick, of the Anne period, with centre and wings making three sides of a quadrangle; a stately old house, lying remote from the high-road, and surrounded by pleasure-grounds and park—the latter somewhat flat and dreary, but on a high level, with glimpses of a fine landscape here and there through a break in the wood. The house had belonged to a law-lord of the Augustan age of good Queen Anne; a once famous law-lord, whose portrait in wig and state-robes looked down from the panelled walls, and with divers other effigies of his wife and children went among the fixtures of the house, and was flung into the bargain on very easy terms, among crystal chandeliers, antique fenders and fire-irons, shutter-bells, and other conveniences of a bygone age. From the law-lord the mansion had descended to a wholesale grocer of the Sir-Baalam type, who thought 'two puddings' luxuries, and rolled ponderously to Mincing-lane every day in his glass coach. Then came an Anglo-Indian colonel, enriched by the plunder of silver-gated cities and Brahminical temples, who held high-jinks in the old house, and ended by throwing himself from an upper window in a fit of delirium tremens. This helped to give the house a bad name, and together with its curiously isolated position, remote from all modes of conveyance — an extreme inconvenience in an age when everybody requires to be conveyed—tended to depress its market value; whereupon it was bought a dead bargain by a speculative solicitor, who tried to let it for some years without success, during which period the inhabitants of Hetheridge, a little village half a mile distant, were confirmed in their conviction that Hetheridge Hall, the mansion in question, was the favourite resort of

> 'Hags, ghosts, and sprites
> That haunt the nights.'

In due time, however, the place came under the

notice of Dr. Cameron, who, as his patients increased in number, required a larger mansion than that in which his father had begun business, and who, finding in Hetheridge and its hall a situation and an abode at once eligible and inexpensive, made haste to secure house and grounds on a long lease, getting the portraits of the law-lord and his olive-branches flung in for an old song, as well as grounds furnished with some of the finest specimens of the fir tribe in the county of Herts.

So the noble music-room, where the bewigged and bepowdered family of the law-lord smirked and simpered on the panelled walls, and where the law-lord himself had entertained the élite of the country-side with stately old-fashioned hospitality, was now given up to the weekly junkettings of ladies and gentlemen of more or less disordered intellect; ladies upon whose head-gear, and gentlemen upon whose collars and cravats, eccentricity had set its seal. Here once a week throughout the slow long winter the doctor's patients pranced and capered through First Sets and Lancers and Caledonians; while the younger and more fashionable among them even essayed round dances. Here, in full view of those stately effigies of the patch-and-powder period, mild refreshment in the way of white-wine negus and raspberry-jam tarts was dispensed between nine o'clock and ten; when the junketters dispersed more or less unwillingly to their several chambers, under close guard of nurses and keepers, who drove them along passages and up staircases like a flock of sheep.

The traveller, lingering a few moments by the park fence to look down the long straight avenue at the grim red façade of Hetheridge Hall, was apt, knowing the story of the place, to fancy dire scenes of horror within those solid old walls: secret dungeon chambers underground, in which wretched creatures, forgotten by all the world except one brutal guardian, languished in sempiternal darkness, chained to a damp black wall, against which the slimy rats pushed noiselessly to fight for the madman's scanty meal; dreary windowless rooms in the heart of the house, approached by secret passages known of but by a few, where pale white-haired women pined in a life-long silence. But there were neither *robora* nor *piombi* in Dr. Cameron's prosperous and comfortable establishment; and the only horrors within that melancholy mansion were the gloomy thoughts of those among its occupants who were not quite mad enough to be unconscious of their state; or the black despair of those in whom madness was a thing of violence and terror, a ceaseless fever of the brain, like a caldron for ever at boiling-point, full of fancies grim and loathsome as the constituents of a witch's hell-broth.

Happily for the doctor there was a good deal of comfortable easy-going lunacy in his establishment: patients who liked their dinner, and kept up their spirits by quarrelling with each other and reviling their nurses. Some of these custodians were amiable young women enough, and really kind to their charges; but there was another class of attendants who, finding life in an asylum rather a dull business, took it out of the patients, and acquired a diabolical skill in the administration of sly pinches and invisible squeezes in public; while in private their mode of remonstrance with a refractory or fretful patient took the more open form of bangs and kicks. Any bruises or abrasions resulting from this rough-and-ready style of argument were easily accounted for as having been self-inflicted by the patient, 'poor thing.'

The doctor was a man of considerable benevolence, who conducted his house on a liberal scale, gave his patients airy rooms, ample service, and good living; and only failed to secure them from the possibility of ill-usage for the simple reason that he was not ubiquitous. He did not live at Hetheridge, but drove down from the West-end once or twice a week in his brougham, saw a few particular cases, smiled his soothing smile upon the victims of mental delusion, dexterously fenced those strange direct questions which madness is apt to put to its guardian, walked through the public rooms, made a good many inquiries, looked about him in a general way, took a chop and a glass or two of dry sherry with his subordinate—the medical superintendent at Hetheridge —and then went back to his metropolitan practice, which was a large one.

In this strange abode Elizabeth awoke one morning from a long troubled dream of swift journeying through the land, bound like a captive in a corner of the railway carriage; for had she not resisted this transit, opposing her sudden removal from Slogh-na-Dyack with what little force she had? whereby the physician, kindly as his nature was, felt himself called upon to exercise his authority with a certain severity of aspect, and to treat Lady Paulyn as a naughty child requiring nursery discipline.

Darker than the darkest dream that ever visited the couch of fever was that rapid journey from north to south. The swiftness of the transit was in itself an agony to that enfeebled brain; the perpetual monotonous thump of the engine, like the throbbing of some giant heart beating itself to death; the ceaseless shifting of the landscape—moor and mountain, valley and wood flitting past behind the blinding rain, like shadows moving in a phantom world; all these things were torment to that distracted mind. No warning of the intended journey had been given to the patient, no hint of impending change in her mode of life; for doctors and nurses alike concurred in treating her as if she had been a sick child. From the hour in which hallucination set in, this infantine treatment had been religiously observed. The possibility of a bright intellect struggling in an agony of perplexed thought behind the dim clouds that obscured it was utterly ignored. Because the patient thought wrongly upon some points, she was set down at once as incapable of reasonable thought upon any point. Left in the dismal blankness of isolation—no friendly word whispered in her ear, no tidings of the outer world permitted to dispute the dominion of wild imaginings—her weakened brain had been wearied by perpetual wonder at her own state, and why she was thus cut off from all communion with her kind.

On the morning of the journey she had been dressed like a child who is taken for an airing, her travelling dress hustled upon her by the nurse's impatient hands, dragged down the stairs against her will—protesting vehemently, in wildest despair, as if moved by some prophetic sense of impending doom. Then came a dream-like apathy, in which thought was not, only the acute agony of shattered nerves.

For some time after her arrival at Hetheridge Park, Lady Paulyn was pronounced unfit for the social circle, as there represented by a small assemblage of ladies and gentlemen of various habits and opinions, whom the world, as represented by doctors and commissioners of lunacy, had agreed in pronouncing of unsound mind. They were not, on the whole, widely different from other ladies and gentlemen, nor did their lunacy exhibit those salient points which afford material for the pen of a Warren or a Gilbert; in fact, they did little to distinguish themselves from the vulgar herd of the sane.

They were a shade more disagreeable than the outside world, or exhibited their various ill-tempers more freely; grumbled a great deal upon every possible subject, and each pursued his or her line of thought without reference to external circumstances, with a harmless egotism not uncommon even in the outer world.

But to these specimens of the later stage of Dr. Cameron's process, which were in a manner the bedded-out plants of his collection, removed from the forcing-house or the hotbed of solitary confinement into the open, Lady Paulyn was not yet considered fit to be introduced. Such at least was the opinion of Dr. Cameron and the house surgeon, who took their opinions from the nurses. Their own visits to Lady Paulyn's rooms only showed them a motionless figure in an arm-chair, with pale dejected face, and loosened hair tossed back from a weary-looking brow; a haggard face, and wild tearless eyes which gazed at them wonderingly out of a dream-world.

The system in this case was naturally the system usual in all other cases; what physician could chop and change his treatment to suit the idiosyncrasies of every new patient? The same smoothing smile which Dr. Cameron, like the sun which shines alike upon the just and the unjust, shed upon a crazy stock-broker whose mental balance had tottered in unison with his balance at his banker's, under the cumulative burden of contango, he shed also upon Lady Paulyn. The gentle gesture with which he smoothed the roughened locks of the wealthy grocer's wife, who had succumbed to a too devoted attention to the wine-and-spirit department of her husband's business, was the same touch, half patronising, half caressing, which he laid like a good man's blessing upon Elizabeth's fevered forehead. He had even a little sympathetic murmur, a faint humming, as of a benevolent bee, which he bestowed alike upon all first-class patients. He perhaps hummed a trifle less for the second-class boarders, but even for them he had kindly pitying smiles, but always as of a superior order of being, whose brain had been constructed upon quite another model, and was altogether a different kind of machine, not by any possibility to be disorganised.

Dr. Cameron, devoting five minutes twice a week or so to this very interesting case, was greeted by the patient only with a despairing silence and mute wondering looks from troubled eyes,—wonder at this period predominating over every other sensation—wonder why she was in that place; why he, Malcolm, had so utterly deserted her; why all her surroundings had undergone a change so sudden and complete that it seemed to her as if she was an infant newly born into a new world—wonder which was mute, for when she tried to speak strange words came, and the power of language seemed to have left her, except in spasmodic outbursts of complaint, complaint addressed to the bare walls or to her adamantine nurses. Dr. Cameron seeing her in this state, and being duly informed by loquacious nurses that Lady Paulyn was violent and hysterical, began to think the chances of speedy cure more than doubtful. The patient talked to herself a great deal, her nurses told him, and obstinately refused to sleep, in which peculiar temper she was the worst subject they had ever had to deal with.

'We don't get a wink of sleep for hours at a stretch,' complained Nurse Barber, of the grenadier aspect. 'Talking to herself all night long, drumming with her fingers on the wall, and that restless! Turn and turn and toss and toss from side to side, and sigh and moan in a way that goes to your very marrow! I think for troublesomeness she's about the worst patient I ever laid eyes on.'

'Does she ever speak of her husband now?' asked the doctor, inquiring for some token of awakening memory.

'Lord bless you, no, sir; and if we say anything about him, stands us out, up hill and down dale, that there's no such person, and that she never was married. Once when I mentioned his name, thinkin' as that might bring her to reason, she looked at me with her foolish smile, twisting and untwisting her hair round her fingers all the time, and said "Poor Lord Paulyn! Yes, he was in love with me once, poor fellow! But that's all over. I was true to Malcolm." As to the way she carries on about that Malcolm, it's downright wicked.'

So Dr. Cameron looked kindly at the troublesome patient, hummed and ha'd a little in his mild way, which meant that he could make nothing of her, murmured something professional to himself about cerebral disturbance, like a clock which strikes in an empty room from the mere habit of striking, and departed, knowing just as much about that curious mystery the human mind in this case as he knew in the case of the drunken grocer's wife, or the demented stockjobber, prescribing almost exactly the same treatment, with a little difference as to diet perhaps, since this was a more delicate organisation—Roussillon instead of bottled stout, the breast of a chicken instead of a rumpsteak—departed, and left Elizabeth in the utter darkness of a lonely room and in the power of the nurses she abhorred.

The lottery of nurses is not unlike that lottery to which some atrabilious misogynist has compared marriage. It is like dipping for a single eel in a bag of snakes. Elizabeth's first draw had resulted in snakes. Her two nurses were first the grenadier woman, with the muscles of a gladiator, not a badly-disposed person perhaps, could one have arrived at the motive principle of her nature, but using her enormous strength half unconsciously, and having a fixed opinion that physical force was the only treatment for a mind askew; secondly, a vain pretty girl, who enjoyed a flirtation with a keeper or gentlemanly lunatic on the high-road to recovery better than the solitude of the patient's chamber, who had adopted the position of madhouse nurse because it paid better than pleasanter modes of industry, and who wreaked her disgust for her calling upon the subject of her care. She was morally worse than the grenadier, heartless and shallow beyond all measure, and maliciously gratified at having a lady at her mercy.

Thus followed the long days and the longer nights; nights for the greater part utterly without sleep, long watches in the dim light of the night-lamp, watches through which all the imps and demons of madness held their horrid Sabbath in that one unresting brain; nights in which the patient's mind was like a rudderless ship driven thousands of miles out of her course, or like a star that has been loosed from its natural station in heaven to reel tempest-driven through infinite space. Who dare follow the thoughts of that distracted brain, the inextricable tangle of waking dreams and shreds of memory, going back to childhood's cloudiest recollections of a world that seemed sweeter than the world known in later years? Nor were those silent nights voiceless for her. Voices that she loved spoke to her from the corridor outside

her door, only divided from her by that fatal locked
door. Sometimes it was her mother's gentle half-
plaintive tone, as of one who had always found life a
thing to grumble at; sometimes her baby's tiny voice
calling with his first broken word, the tender cry she
had been so proud to hear; sometimes her father's
genial tones; for in this long dream of madness death
was not. But oftenest of all came the voice of Malcolm Forde. He was always near her, shielding
and consoling her. There were nights when he would
not speak, but she was not the less convinced of his
presence. She knelt by that cruel door in the dead
of the night—while the nurses, stretched grimly on
their truckle-beds, kept guard over her as they slept
—and laid her head against the panel, and felt that
her loved ones were near her; felt as if their very
breath shed a gentle warmth through the magnetic
wood, and melted the ice at her heavy heart. She
was as certain of their vicinity as she had ever been
of any fact in her life. She never doubted, never
questioned how they had come there, wondered at
nothing except why she was separated from them,
and this severance she came by and by to ascribe to
the settled enmity of her nurses.

With the gray light of morning that dream would
vanish, and give place to another fancy, or sometimes

to a period of dull apathy, an absolute blank, in which perhaps the brain rested after its nightly fever. She was quiet enough in the day, the nurses admitted to each other, whereby they contrived to steal various hours for their own amusements, gossip or flirtation as the case might be, while the patient sat alone and stared at the fire, whose dangerous properties were guarded by a large wire screen. Against this screen Elizabeth leant, and looked into the fire, which seemed the most sympathetic thing in her narrow world, and struck wild chords on the wires of the guard, and imagined the music that should have answered to her touch, and even played some simple melody of days gone by—' Vedrai carino,' or ' Voi che sapéte.'

No one essayed to help her back to sense and memory. The doctors came and looked at her, and patted her on the head, and passed from before her sight like the shifting shadows of a magic-lantern, and had about as much meaning for her. No one tried to awaken her senses from their long dream with books or genial talk, with music, or pictures, or flowers, or any of those familiar things that might have touched the mystic chords of memory. There was a certain routine for all patients at Hetheridge Hall, where madness was cured, or taken care of, upon a wholesale system, not admitting of minute differences. A comfortable open carriage was maintained for the use of the first-class patients, and these, when pronounced well enough for such indulgence, were allowed to commune with nature daily during an hour's drive, generally on the same turnpike-road. A glimpse of the outer world which raised strange vague longings in some distracted minds, whilst for other more sluggish spirits the wide wintry landscape and the distant dome of St. Paul's, seen dimly athwart a blue-gray cloud, seemed no more than a picture flashed before their troubled eyes—a picture of fields and hedgerows and sky and cloud dimly remembered in some former stage of existence.

During the first six weeks of her residence at Hetheridge—time of which the patient herself kept no count, but which seemed rather a vast blank interval, a dismal pause wherein life came to a standstill, than so many days and nights—Lady Paulyn was pronounced too weak for out-of-door exercise of any kind whatever, and in this period she scarcely saw the sky. It was there certainly—the blue vault of heaven—visible from the upper part of her window, the lower half being kept closely shuttered lest she should do herself a mischief; for Nurse Barber remembered and dwelt upon that little episode at

Slogh-na-Dyack when she had sought to force herself out of the window. The sky was there, within reach of her dull eyes, and she did not look up at it. Her brain was a medley of old thoughts, a chaos of many-coloured scraps and shreds, like a good housekeeper's rag-bag. All her married life—with its social triumphs, its unbroken brilliancy, its splendour and extravagance—was as if it had never been; and young memories, childish fancies, and the days when her first and only love ripened into passion, usurped her mind. Madness, which in its worst folly has a curious tendency to hit upon universal truths, revealed the unquenchable power of a first poetic love —a love which, pure as the vestal's sacred fire, burns with its quiet light through all the storms of life, and grows brighter as the pilgrim's path descends the valley where the shadows thicken on the border-land of life and death.

CHAPTER XIII.

> 'Hast thou no care of me? Shall I abide
> In this dull world, which in thy absence is
> No better than a sty?'

TONGATABOO and Taheiti—or the Tongataboo and Taheiti of the day—had to wait the return of their pastor. Savage chieftains, holding council in the domestic seclusion of their matting with their wives and families, could but lament the absence of that white-skinned teacher whom at his first coming they had been disposed to treat as a god. That autumn-tide did not see Malcolm Forde's return to the South-Sea Islands. For a little while at least even duty must be in abeyance, his place must wait for him. The society for which he had worked knew him well enough to know that he was thoroughly in earnest—that he would return in due time, and complete the labour he had begun, and widen the area of his labours, and faint not until Death should say to him, 'Thus far, and no farther, shalt thou journey, O pilgrim and messenger!'

Meanwhile he stayed in England to do something very near his heart, to watch and pray for the woman he loved, and whom, as it seemed, all the world except himself had abandoned to bitterest fate. But for him Gertrude Luttrell would have yielded helplessly, nervelessly, almost placidly to the force of circumstances—would have meekly accepted the fact that her sister had been transferred to a lunatic asylum as a melancholy necessity, against which there could be no appeal, beyond which there could be but the smallest margin for hope.

But Malcolm Forde was not inclined to take things so patiently. He came straightway to London with Miss Luttrell, saw Mrs. Chevenix, whose malady—chronic neuralgia—seemed hardly so severe or tangible an affliction as to justify her refusal to come to her niece's rescue, and who, in this sad crisis of her favourite niece's life, had little help of any kind to offer, and seemed chiefly tormented by a melancholy foreboding that *it*, meaning Elizabeth's madness, would get into the papers.

'Everything does get into the papers sooner or later,' she said despondently. 'I'm sure there's no such thing as the sanctity of private life for people of position. I shall never take up my *Morning Post* without a shudder from this time forward.'

'Had we not better think of how we are to save your niece from the anguish of her present situation rather than of keeping the fact out of the *Morning Post?*' said Mr. Forde. 'It might be necessary even for us to appeal to the press for help, if we found no other way of rescuing her.'

'O Mr. Forde!' moaned Mrs. Chevenix, applying herself mechanically to her scent-bottle; 'don't pray talk about the anguish of her situation. We have no reason to suppose that she is unhappy. With my nephew Lord Paulyn's splendid income she would, of course, be sure of the very highest form of treatment; every advantage which wealth could provide.'

'We will take that for ganted, if you like. But she is in the hands of strangers, and even her sister does not know where or with whom. The fitful fever of the brain which succeeded fever of the body has been set down as madness, and in that state of mental exaltation—every sense intensified, her capacity for suffering increased twentyfold—she has been handed over to strangers, whose interests will be best served by her permanent estrangement. Say that they are conscientious and will do their best to cure her, will the best they can do counterbalance the horror of that sudden removal to an entirely strange place, and the banishment of every human creature and every object with which she was familiar? Is not such a shock eminently calculated to turn temporary hallucination into life-long madness? I am almost distracted when I think of what has been done!' cried Malcolm, starting from his chair, and pacing the Eaton-place drawing-room—the room which seemed destined only to witness his misery.

Mrs. Chevenix sighed, and again sought relief from the scent-bottle, first from one end and then the other, as if in aromatic vinegar there might lurk a virtue that was not in sal volatile.

'The first thing to be done,' said Malcolm, coming to a standstill by the writing-table, at which Gertrude sat helpless, those perpetual tears standing in her eyes—she had done nothing but shed those two slow languid tears since she left Slogh-na-Dyack, as if, having produced these silent evidences of feeling, she had done her duty to her sister,—'the first thing to be done is for Miss Luttrell to write to Lord Paulyn, requesting to be immediately informed of the place to which her sister has been taken, and the people to whom she has been intrusted. You had better write the letter in duplicate, Miss Luttrell, and address one copy to Park-lane, and the other to Slogh-na-Dyack.'

Miss Luttrell endeavoured to obey, with a sheep-like meekness, but finding her absolutely incapable of framing a sentence, Mr. Forde himself dictated the letter, which was brief and decisive, ending with the formal request, 'Be good enough to telegraph an immediate reply.'

It was also at Mr. Forde's suggestion that Miss Luttrell took up her abode in her aunt's house until such time as she should be better informed about her sister's fate.

Having done this, and feeling, with supreme pain, that there was little more he could do, Mr. Forde went to his solicitor in Lincoln's-inn-fields, and took counsel with him upon the legal aspect of Lady Paulyn's position. The lawyer's opinion was not particularly cheering. Elizabeth's husband was her natural guardian. With the sanction of the Commissioners in Lunacy, he could place her in whatever licensed establishment he pleased. Her sisters and her aunt counted for very little in her life.

No reply to Gertrude's letter came in the shape of a telegram; but three days after the letter had been sent—days of intolerable length for Malcolm Forde —there came a curt scrawl from the Viscount, informing his 'Dear Miss Luttrell' that Lady Paulyn had been placed in the care of Dr. Cameron, of Chesterfield-row, and Hetheridge Hall, Herts; that it was quite impossible she could be in better hands; and that, having already suffered so much trouble and annoyance from this unhappy event, he must request that no further letters might be addressed to him upon the subject. He was on the point of starting for Rome, where he meant to winter; his native country having become obnoxious to him. The letter was full of his lordship's personal grievance, and contained not one affectionate or compassionate allusion to his wife.

It contained, however, all that Malcolm Forde wanted to know, the name of the doctor and the madhouse.

He made Gertrude accompany him to Chesterfield-row within half-an-hour of the receipt of the letter. He had taken up his quarters for a few days with an old friend in Cadogan-place, in order to be within five minutes' walk of Mrs. Chevenix's house, and had stipulated that a messenger should bring him immediate tidings of Lord Paulyn's reply. Thus it was that so little time was lost between the arrival of the letter and their interview with Lady Paulyn's physician.

Dr. Cameron was kindness itself; smiled his sweet smile upon Gertrude and her clerical friend; pledged himself to do all that he could do, in reason.

'But really what you ask for, Mr.—Mr. Forde,' with a glance at the cards that had been sent in to him, 'is quite out of the question. I can perfectly understand Miss Luttrell's natural desire to see her sister. But an interview, in the present stage of affairs, is simply impossible.'

'Yet is it not just possible, Dr. Cameron, that the sight of some one whom she has known and loved all her life—a familiar home-face, bringing back old memories—might strike a chord—'

'My dear sir,' exclaimed the doctor in his blandest way, ' that is the very thing we want to avoid; there must be no chords struck yet awhile, the instrument is not strong enough to bear the shock. It is all very well on the stage or in a novel; we are told to believe that a favourite melody is played, a familiar face is seen, and the patient gives a shriek, and recovers his senses in a moment upon the spot. My dear sir, there is no such thing possible. Mental aberration, without positive change in the condition of the brain, is a thing of the rarest occurrence. We have to cure the brain, which we can neither see nor handle, just as we set a broken arm, which we can do what we like with. And the first and most essential step towards recovery is repose, absolute rest. You will understand, therefore, my dear Miss Luttrell, why

I am compelled to forbid any intrusion upon the tranquil solitude in which our dear patient is now placed.'

'How soon may I see her?' asked Gertrude.

'That is a question beyond my power to answer. All must depend upon her progress towards recovery. If she recovers, which I trust, which I may venture to say I believe, she ultimately will, I shall be happy to let you see her directly I find her mind strong enough to bear the emotion that must be caused by such a meeting. I will not ask you to wait till she is really well, for that naturally will be an affair of time, and at the best rather a long time; but as soon as the brain begins to regain its balance, concurrently with the return of bodily strength, you shall be allowed to see her. Lord Paulyn, who is naturally as anxious as yourself, has resigned himself to the inevitable, and submits to my judgment in this sad affair.'

'He is so far resigned,' said Mr. Forde with some touch of bitterness, 'that he contemplates going abroad, and putting the Channel between himself and his afflicted wife.'

'A step I myself recommended,' replied Dr. Cameron. 'Lord Paulyn has been rather severely shaken by this business, and as he is of an excitable temperament, the consequences to himself might not be without peril.'

The conversation lasted some time longer. Mr. Forde was not easily satisfied. He tried to obtain some definite expression of the physician's opinion. But physicians are not given to definite opinions. Dr. Cameron see-sawed the matter in his most delicate way, said all that was kind about Lady Paulyn, persuaded Miss Luttrell that the best thing she could possibly do would be to go back to Devonshire and there quietly wait for tidings of her sister's recovery, and then politely dismissed his visitors, who had really usurped a good deal of his valuable morning, while patients with their fees neatly papered in their waistcoat-pockets were yawning over a three-weeks-old *Illustrated London News*, or a year-old *Quarterly*.

Gertrude left Chesterfield-row sorely dejected in mind, and disposed to take the doctor's advice, and go straight back to the little house in the Borough-bridge-road, where bright fenders and fire-irons and polished tables would be going to rack and ruin in the absence of her supervising eye. She, of old so strong-minded, seemed to have become the weakest and most helpless of womankind.

'It isn't as if I could be any good to Elizabeth,'

she said. 'If I could help her in any way I shouldn't care what sacrifices I made. But Dr. Cameron says I may have to wait for months before he can let me see her, and what will become of the house all that time, with only Diana and Blanche, who have no more idea of looking after things than if they were infants? We shall all be ruined if I don't go back soon.'

'And when you are gone back, if your sister were dying, and Dr. Cameron at the last moment awoke to the idea that she should have some one near her whom she had loved, you will be in Devonshire—too far to be summoned in time to be of any use.'

'But she is not going to die,' cried Gertrude, with a frightened look; 'Dr. Cameron said nothing about her dying.'

'Not directly; but he said she was in a very weak state of health, and a physician seldom says quite all he means. I have seen her, remember, and the change I saw in her was enough to put sad forebodings into my mind. O God, to think of her alone in a madhouse,' he cried, with a little burst of passion, 'the brightest creature that ever lived upon this earth!'

'But they will take the utmost care of her,' said Gertrude tremulously, and with a faint pang of envy, envying Elizabeth even now because Malcolm Forde had loved her, still loved her, perhaps, for was not this keen anxiety more than simple Christian charity? 'Dr. Cameron told us that; and she will have every comfort—every luxury—a carriage at her disposal when she is well enough to use it.'

'Every comfort—every luxury! Do you think your sister cares for comforts and luxuries in a prison? Her proud free spirit might have found happiness on a desert island. Bondage has strangled it—the bondage of a fatal marriage—and now the bondage of a madhouse. Gertrude, when I think of the past I am almost mad. If I had not been the proudest fool that ever lived, all this might have been prevented. 'My darling,' he murmured softly, 'that bright mind should never have gone astray had I had the keeping of it.'

He grew calmer presently, and discussed things quietly with Gertrude, who, shamed out of her small worldliness by his deeper feeling, agreed to remain in Eaton-place so long as aunt Chevenix would shelter her there; or, if need were, to take a modest lodging nearer her sister's prison-house, and to let fenders, fire-irons, and even the family tea-kettle, enfolded in baize and cunningly secreted under the best bed, take care of themselves.

CHAPTER XIV.

> 'Did I speak once angrily, all the drear days
> You lived, you woman I loved so well,
> Who married the other? Blame or praise,
> Where was the use then? Time would tell,
> And the end declare what man for you,
> What woman for me, was the choice of God.'

THROUGH the dull days of November, into the dreary mid-winter, Malcolm Forde lived in the little village of Hetheridge, and in his lonely walks every day, and often twice a day, beheld the walls that shut Elizabeth from all the outer world. Christmas had come and gone—a strangely quiet Christmas—and he had not yet seen Dr. Cameron's patient, though he had been favoured with several brief interviews with the doctor, who had cheered him lately with the intelligence that all was going well; there had been lately decided signs of improvement; the patient had been allowed to mingle a little with the sanest among her fellow patients, had assisted at their little weekly dance, though that modest festival had not appeared to make much impression upon her; she had stared at the long lighted music room and the people dancing in smartened morning-dress and various-coloured gloves wonderingly, and had asked if it were a servants' ball. But she had been latterly more amenable to reason; the nurses complained less of her violence; she had been taken for an airing in the grounds on fine days, and would go out in the carriage as soon as the weather grew a little milder. Altogether, the account was cheering, and Mr. Forde was fain to be satisfied, and to thank God for so much mercy in answer to his prayers.

He was not quite idle even at Hetheridge, but had made friends with the incumbent of the little rustic church and helped him with his duty, and made himself an awakening influence even in this narrow circle. He visited the poor, and catechised the children on Sunday afternoons, and very much lightened the burden of the perpetual curate of Hetheridge, who was an elderly man with a chronic asthma. This work, and long hours of quiet study deep into the winter's night, made his life tolerable to him—made it easy to wait and watch and hope for the hour of Elizabeth's recovery.

And when she should have recovered — what then?

Why, then she would go back to her husband, and to her old worldly life, most likely, and grow weary of it again. O, no, he would not believe this. He would hope that by God's blessing this dismal warning would not have been sent in vain, that she would begin an entirely new life, a life of unselfishness and good works, a life brightened by faith and prayer, a life which should be her apprenticeship to Christianity, her education for the world to come.

This was what he hoped for, this was the end to which he looked forward, after that blessed day when she should stand before him in her right mind.

This consummation seemed to be a little nearer by and by, when Dr. Cameron said, that if Miss Luttrell would procure a line from Lord Paulyn giving his consent to an interview with the patient, he, the doctor, would sanction such an interview in the course of the following week.

'Do you mean to say that it is necessary to obtain Lord Paulyn's consent before his afflicted wife can be allowed to see her own sister, her nearest surviving relative?' asked Malcolm, with a touch of indignation.

'Unquestionably, my dear sir,' answered the doctor. 'Lord Paulyn placed this dear lady in my care, and I have no right to permit her to see any one, even her nearest-of-kin, until I am certain of his approval. The bond between man and wife, my dear sir—as I need hardly suggest to a gentleman of your sacred calling—is above all other ties.'

'Yes; and as interpreted by the common law of England is sometimes a curious bondage,' said Mr. Forde bitterly; 'separating a woman from all that was dear to her in the past, encompassing her life with a boundary which no one shall cross—let her suffer what she may—except her sufferings assume that special shape which the makers of the divorce-law have taken into consideration. Thus, a man may break his wife's heart, but must not break her bones, in the presence of witnesses.'

'Lord Paulyn has been a most devoted husband, I believe,' said Dr. Cameron, with a disapproving air.

'I have no reason to believe otherwise. Only it seems rather hard that your patient cannot see her sister without her husband's permission. It is taking no account of all her past life. And there may be some delay in obtaining this consent, unless you can give Miss Luttrell her brother-in-law's address.'

'Lord Paulyn was in Rome when I last heard from him,' replied Dr. Cameron, with an agreeable recollection of his lordship's communication, which had been merely an envelope enclosing a cheque. 'If it will save Miss Luttrell trouble, I shall be happy to write to him myself. Of course such an appeal to his wishes is a mere point of ceremony, but one which I feel myself bound to observe.'

'You are very good. Yes, if you will write I am sure Miss Luttrell will be obliged to you.'

It was settled therefore that Dr. Cameron should apply for the required permission, and Gertrude must await the answer to his letter, however tardily Lord Paulyn might reply.

The week spoken of by the physician came and went, and he acknowledged that his patient was now well enough to see her sister, but there was no answer from Rome.

The Viscount had gone elsewhither, perhaps, and the doctor's letter was following by the slow foreign stages.

This delay seemed a hard thing to Malcolm Forde, almost harder to bear than the long period of doubt and fear, when at each new visit to the physician he had dreaded to hear the patient pronounced incurable. Now when God had given her back to them—for these first slow signs of improvement he accepted as the promise of speedy cure—man interposed with his petty forms and ceremonies, and said,

'She shall languish alone; the slow dawn of sense shall show her nothing but strange faces; the first glimmer of awakening reason shall find her in loneliness and abandonment; the first thought her mind shall shape shall be to think herself forgotten by all her little world, put away from them like a leper, to live or die as God pleases, without their love or their help.'

It was in vain that he pleaded with Dr. Cameron.

'I would rather wait for the letter,' the kind-hearted physician said in his mild gentlemanlike way. 'A little delay will do no harm. The mind is certainly recovering its balance, and I hope great things from the return of mild weather. I have given Lady Paulyn new apartments — those small changes are sometimes beneficial—and a piano; the exciting tendency of music was a point to be avoided until now; and I have changed her nurses. Poor thing, she fancied the last were unkind; the merest delusion, as they were women of the highest character, and peculiarly skilled in their avocation.'

Another week went by, and there was still no communication from Lord Paulyn. Dr. Cameron had written again, at Mr. Forde's earnest request, and Gertrude had also written, but there was no answer to either letter. Malcolm Forde paced the lonely road outside the fences of Hetheridge Park for hours together in the dull February afternoons, saw the firelight shining from the distant windows of the Hall, which looked a comfortable mansion as its many lattices shone out upon the wintry dusk; a mansion in which one could fancy happy home-like scenes; the patter of childish feet on polished oak staircases, fresh young voices singing old ballads in the gloaming; lovers snatching brief glimpses of Paradise in shadowy corridors, from the light touch of a little hand or the shy murmur of two rosy lips; all sweet things that wait upon youth and hope and love, instead of madmen's disjointed dreams, and the tramping to and fro of weary feet that know not whither they would go.

He could only watch and wait and hope and pray, pray that the return of reason might restore her to peace and a calmer loftier frame of mind than she had ever known yet. For his own part he had never even hinted a wish to see her. Indeed, he did hardly desire to see that too lovely face again, most lovely to him even in its decay. It would be enough for him to hear of her from Gertrude; enough for him to have secured her the consolation of a sister's companionship; and by and by, when she was restored to health and released from her captivity—a captivity which should not last an hour longer than was necessary, Dr. Cameron assured him—he could go back to his distant vineyard, with his soul at peace. In the mean time it was his duty to watch for her and care for her, as a brother might have done.

CHAPTER XV.

> 'Look on me! There is an order
> Of mortals on the earth, who do become
> Old in their youth, and die ere middle age,
> Without the violence of warlike death;
> Some perishing of pleasure—some of study—
> Some worn with toil—some of mere weariness—
> Some of disease—and some insanity—
> And some of wither'd, or of broken hearts;
> For this last is a malady which slays
> More than are number'd in the lists of Fate,
> Taking all shapes, and bearing many names.'

ELIZABETH was better. The time had come when she could shape her thoughts into words; when Dr. Cameron's kind face, smiling gently at her, had become something more than a picture; when it had ceased also to recall to her first one person, then another, faintly remembered among the hazy crowd of former acquaintance, the people she had known in the Park-lane period of her life. The time had come at last when she knew him as her custodian; though why he should be so, she knew not, nor yet the meaning of her imprisonment. But he seemed to her a person in authority, and to him she appealed against her nurses, telling him that they had been cruel to her, more cruel than words could speak, especially her words, poor soul! which came tremulously from the pale lips, and were apt to shape disjointed phrases. The nurses strenuously denied the truth of this accusation; whereupon Dr. Cameron gently shook his head, as who should say, 'Poor soul, poor soul! we know how much significance to attach to her complaints; but we may as well humour her.' So Nurse Barber and Nurse Lucas were passed on to another patient in the preliminary and violent stage, and Lady Paulyn was now so fortunate as to be committed to the care of a soft-hearted low-voiced little woman who had none of the vices of the Gamp sisterhood. This change, and a change in her apartments to rooms with a southern aspect, looking out upon a flower-garden, produced a favourable effect. The patient began to sleep a little at night, awoke from wild dreams of the past, recognised the blank lonely present, and knew that she was severed from all she had ever loved; knew that her dead were verily dead, and that the voices she had heard in all those long winter nights had been only dream voices.

Memory was slow to return, and the power of consecutive thought. Ideas flashed across her brain like lightning, and ideas that were for the greater part false. Her mind was like a diamond-cut crystal reflecting gleams of many-coloured light, or like a kaleidoscope in which thought was for ever running from one form into another. Her brain was never quiet. It thought and thought, and invented and imagined, but rarely remembered, or only remembered the remote past; and even in those memories fact was mixed with fiction. Books that had impressed her long ago were as much a portion of her life as the actual events of the past; and even in her broken memories of books, imagination bewildered and deceived her. There were poems of Byron's, the 'Giaour,' the 'Prisoner of Chillon,' which in her girlhood she had been able to repeat from the first line to the last. She could remember a line here and there now, and murmured it to herself sadly, again and again. And out of this grew a fancy that she had known Byron, that she had met him in Italy and in Greece, had stood upon the sea-shore at Lerici when the white-sailed bark that held genius and Shelley vanished from the storm-swept waters. This and a hundred other such fancies filled her brain. She left off thinking of Malcolm Forde, to think of beings she had never known, creatures of her wild imagining.

Left to the companionship of a nurse whose ideas rarely soared above the question of turning a last winter's gown, or putting new ribbon on an old bonnet, invention supplied the place of society. She conversed with phantoms, held mysterious communion with shadows. Were there not people outside her window for whom she had a secret code of signals? Did she not laugh to herself sometimes at the thought of how she cheated her custodians?

Sometimes she was gay with a feverish gaiety, at other times melancholy to despair, weeping a rain of tears without knowing why she wept. Dr. Cameron being informed of these melancholy fits, suggested that she should mix more freely with the other patients; that she should spend an hour or two in the drawing-room with the milder cases, and even attend the weekly soirées, and derive gladness from the Lancers and Caledonians. So one sunny morning, when the aspect of Nature, even in her winter garment, was cheerful, Lady Paulyn's nurse led her down to the drawing-room, and left her there alone on an ottoman near the fireplace, while all the milder cases stared at her with a dreamy indifferent stare, but not without some glimmer of sane superciliousness.

The drawing-room was long and spacious, with

a fireplace at each end, oak panelling and family portraits, a room that did really seem a little too good even for the milder cases, who were hardly up to oak panelling or the Sir Joshua Reynolds' school of portraiture. The windows were high and wide, and the sun shone in upon the scattered figures, not grouped about either of the fireplaces, but scattered about the length and breadth of the room, each as remote as possible from her companions, and all idle. There they sat, solitary among numbers, all staring straight before them after that one brief survey of Elizabeth—some talking to themselves in a dreamy monotonous way, others silent.

Elizabeth looked round her wonderingly. What were they? Guests in a country house? What a strange look they had, dressed not unlike other people, with faces like the faces of the rest of womankind so far as actual feature went, yet with so curious a stamp upon every countenance and every figure, and some minute eccentricity in every dress! And then that low sullen muttering—solitary-looking women complaining to themselves in a hopeless subdued manner; then suddenly that low sound of complaint swelled to a little burst of clamour, half-a-dozen shrill voices raised at the same instant, a discordant noise as of cats quarrelling, which was hushed as suddenly at the behest of a clever-looking little woman, dressed in black, who walked quickly up and down the room remonstrating.

There was an open piano near the fireplace. Elizabeth sat down before it presently and began to play—dreamily—as if awakening reason found a vague voice in music. But she had hardly played a dozen bars when a tall gaunt-looking woman, in brown and yellow, came up to her and pulled her away from the piano.

'I'll have no more of your noise,' she said; 'you're always at it, and I won't stand it any longer.'

'But I never saw you before to-day,' pleaded Elizabeth, looking at her with innocent wondering eyes—eyes that had grown childlike in that long slumber of the mind. 'I can't have annoyed you before to-day.'

'Stuff and nonsense! You have annoyed me; you're a detestable nuisance. I won't have that piano touched. First and foremost, it's my property—'

'Come, come, Mrs. Sloper,' said the little woman in black, who occupied the onerous post of matron in this part of the establishment. 'You mustn't be naughty. You've been very naughty all this morning, and I shall really have to complain to Mr. Burley.'

Mr. Burley was the resident medical man, a gentleman who enjoyed the privilege of daily intercourse with the cases, and had to do a good deal of mild flirtation with the first-class lady patients, each of whom fancied she had a peculiar right to the doctor's attention.

Elizabeth wondered a little to hear a broad-shouldered female, on the wrong side of forty, reproved for naughtiness, in the kind of tone usually addressed to a child of six. It was strange, but no stranger than the rest of her new life. There were some books on the table by the fireplace, the first books she had seen since her illness. She seized upon them eagerly, and began to turn the leaves, and look at the pictures. They seemed to speak to her, to be full of secret messages from some one she had loved. Who was it she had once loved so dearly? She could not even remember his name.

'O, mamma, mamma, mamma!' moaned a lady in an arm-chair on the opposite side of the hearth; a middle-aged lady, stout of build, with pepper-and-salt-coloured hair neatly plaited and tied up with brown ribbons, in the street-door-knocker style, like a school-girl's. 'O, mamma, mamma!' she moaned, lifting her voice with every repetition of her cry; 'take me home to my mamma.'

'Miss Chiffinch,' said the matron, 'you really must not go on so; you disturb everybody, and it is exceedingly silly to talk like that. Your mamma has been dead for the last twenty years.'

'You fool!' replied Miss Chiffinch, with ineffable scorn; 'as if I didn't know that as well as you.' And then resumed her cuckoo cry, 'O, mamma, mamma!'

One young woman, with straight brown hair hanging down her back, walked about the room in a meandering kind of way, trying to fasten herself upon somebody, like the little boy who wanted the brute creation to play with him; and, like that idle child, was rejected by all. She came up to Elizabeth presently, as if hoping to obtain sympathy from a new arrival.

'My sisters are so 'appy,' she said; 'so 'appy. They're all at 'ome, and they do enjoy themselves so; they're as 'appy as the day is long. Don't you think they'd let me go 'ome? I do so want to go 'ome; my sisters are so 'appy.'

'Why don't you try to employ yourself, Miss Pocock,' demanded the busy little matron, who was always knitting a stocking, and whose needles flew as she walked up and down the room or remonstrated with her charges. 'You'd get well as soon again if you'd try to do something; I'll give you some plain work, if you like; anything would be better than roaming about like that, worrying everybody.'

'O, Mrs. Dawlings, do let me go 'ome,' pleaded Miss Pocock, in her drawling tone; 'my sisters are so 'appy. O, dear Mr. Burley,' this with a little gush as she espied the house doctor entering by a door near at hand, '*do* let me go 'ome. I'll be so grateful, and I'll be so good to father, and never be troublesome any more. My sisters are *so* 'appy!'

'You should have behaved better when you *were* at home,' said Mr. Burley, with friendly candour. 'There, go along,' as Miss Pocock hung upon his arm affectionately, 'and try to get well; get some needlework, and sit down and keep yourself quiet.' With which scientific advice Mr. Burley walked on and looked at the other patients, with a cool cursory glance at each; as if they had been a flock of sheep, and he, their shepherd, only wanted to assure himself he had the right number.

This was the ladies' drawing-room; the gentlemen had their own apartments in the east wing. The second-class patients, male and female, had their apartments in the west wing; and there were private sitting-rooms in abundance for patients not well enough or quiet enough for general society. The majority of these drawing-room cases were old stagers, people who had been in Dr. Cameron's care for years, and were likely to end their lives, contentedly enough perhaps, despite that chronic moaning, under his roof. They were well fed, and living thus publicly under the matron's eye were not much subject to the dominion of cruel nurses. They had comfortable rooms, good fires, weekly high-jinks in the winter, little dances on the lawn in the summer, an annual picnic, and, in short, such small solace as humanity could devise; and the slow dull lives they led here could hardly have been much slower or duller than the lives which some people, in their right mind, lead by choice in a country town.

Elizabeth looked at her fellow patients in a dreamy way; turned the leaves of the books—reading a few lines here and there—the words always assuming a kind of hidden meaning for her, as if they had been mystic messages intended for her eye alone; but when the book was closed she had no memory of anything she had read in it. She dined with the milder cases, male and female, in the public dining-room, at the request of Mr. Burley, who wanted to see the effect of society, even such society as that, as an awakening influence.

Here the cases behaved tolerably enough, though exhibiting the selfishness of poor humanity with an amount of candour which does not obtain in the outside world. There was a good deal of grumbling about the viands, chiefly in an under-tone, and the patients were perpetually remonstrating with the serving-man who administered to their wants, and who had rather a hard time of it. There were even attempts at conversation: Mr. Burley saying a few words in a brisk business-like way now and then at his end of the table, and the matron politely addressing her neighbours at her end. One elderly gentleman, with a limp white cravat and watery blue eyes, fixed upon Elizabeth, and favoured her with an exposition of his theological views. 'You have an intelligent countenance, madam,' he said, 'and I think you are capable of appreciating my ideas. There is a sad want of intellectuality in people here; a profound indifference to those larger questions which— No, Dickson, I will *not* have a waxy potato; how many times must I tell you that there is a conspiracy in this house to give me waxy potatoes! Take the plate away, sir! I was about to observe, madam, that you have an intellectual countenance, and are, I doubt not—' Here Dickson's arrival with his plate again broke the thread of the elderly gentleman's discourse, and he branched off into a complaint against the administration for its unjust distribution of gravy; and then began again, and kept on beginning again with trifling variation of phrase till the end of dinner.

After dinner Jane Howlet, the nurse, bore Elizabeth away to her own apartment; but here she had now a piano, on which she played for hours together all the old dreamy Mendelssohn and Chopin music which she had played long ago in those dull days at the Vicarage when all her life had been a dream of Malcolm Forde. She played now as she had played then, weaving her thoughts into the music; and slowly, slowly, slowly the curtain was lifted, sense and memory came back, until one day she remembered that she was Lord Paulyn's wife, and that there was an impassable gulf between her and the man she loved.

So one morning when Dr. Cameron, going his weekly round, with Mr. Burley in attendance on him, asked her the old question about her husband in his gentle fatherly voice, she no longer looked up at him with vague wonder in her eyes, but looked downward with a sad smile, a smile in which there was thought.

'My husband,' she repeated slowly. 'No, I do not want to see him. Ours was not a happy marriage. He was always very good to me—let me have my own way in most things—only I couldn't be happy with him. I used to think that kind of life—a fine lady's life—must be happiness, but I was punished for my folly. It didn't make *me* happy.'

This was by far the most reasonable speech she had uttered since she left Slogh-na-Dyack, but Dr. Cameron looked at his assistant with a pensive smile. 'Still very rambling,' he murmured, and then he patted Elizabeth's head with his gentlemanly hand. 'You must try to get well, my dear lady,' he said; 'compose yourself, and collect your thoughts, and don't talk too much. And then I shall soon be able to write to your good kind husband and tell him you are better. Don't you think he'll be very pleased to hear that?'

'I don't know,' answered Elizabeth moodily; 'if he cared very much he would hardly have left me here.'

'My dear lady, your coming here was unavoidable. And see what good it has done you!'

'Good!' she cried, with a wild look. 'You don't know what I suffered in that horrible room, locked in, with those brutal women. Good! Why, between them they drove me mad!'

This speech cost Elizabeth a melancholy entry in

the physician's note-book: 'Very little improvement; ideas wild, delusion about nurses continues.'

The weekly festive gatherings, at which she was now permitted to assist, were not enlivening to Lady Paulyn's spirits. She sat on a bench against the wall watching the dancers, who really seemed to enjoy themselves in their divers manners, except Miss Chiffinch, who was not terpsichorean, and who sat in her corner and moaned for her mamma; and Miss Pocock, who, even in the midst of the Caledonians, buttonholed her fellow dancers in order to inform them that her sisters were '*so* 'appy!'

Mr. Burley himself assisted at these weekly dances, in white-kid gloves, and, as long as things went tolerably well, made believe that the dancers were quite up to the mark, and on a level with dancers in the outside world. Everything was done ceremoniously. The orchestra consisted of a harp, fiddle, and clarionet, all played by servants of the establishment. Mr. Burley danced with all the more distinguished ladies; curious-looking matrons in high caps and china-crape shawls, whose gloves were too large for them, but this was a peculiarity of everybody's gloves, being bought for them by the heads of the house with no special reference to size. He asked Elizabeth to dance the First Set with him, but she declined.

'I never dance at servants' balls,' she said; 'it is all very well to look on for half-an-hour, but I should think they would enjoy themselves more if one kept away altogether.'

'But this is not a servants' ball.'

'What is it, then?'

Mr. Burley was rather at a loss for a reply.

'A—a friendly little dance,' he said, 'got up to amuse you all.'

'But it doesn't amuse me at all. I don't know any of these people, they have not been introduced to me. I thought it was a servants' party.'

'O, Mr. Burley, do please let me go 'ome,' exclaimed Miss Pocock, swooping down upon the superintendent. 'I do so want to go 'ome. My sisters are so 'appy.'

'I tell you what it is, Melinda'—Miss Pocock's name was Melinda, and being youthful she was usually addressed by her Christian name—'if you don't behave yourself properly, you shall be sent to bed. Home indeed; why, you'll have to stop here another twelvemonth if you go on bothering everybody like this.'

'O, Mr. Burley! And my sisters are so 'appy. There'll be tarts and negus presently, won't there?'

'Perhaps, if you behave yourself.'

'Then I will. But my sisters are *so* 'appy.'

Mr. Burley pushed her away with a friendly push, and she was presently absorbed in the whirlpool of a set of Lancers, and was informing people of her sisters' happiness to the tune of 'When the heart of a man is oppressed with care.' The house surgeon was more interested in Lady Paulyn than in Miss Melinda Pocock, who was the youngest daughter of an Essex farmer, idle, selfish, greedy, and troublesome, and by no means a profoundly interesting case.

He talked to Elizabeth for a little, talked seriously, and found her answers grow more reasonable as he went on. Did she remember Scotland, and her house there? Yes, she told him, with a shudder. She hated the house, but she loved the country, the hills, and the wide lakes, and the great sea beyond.

'I should like to live out upon those hills alone, all the rest of my life,' she said.

'You must get well, and go back there in the summer.'

'Not to that house; to a cottage among the hills, a cottage of my own, where I could live by myself. I will never go back to that house and the people in it. But why do you all talk to me about getting well? There is nothing the matter with me, or at least only my tiresome cough, which will be well soon enough.'

CHAPTER XVI.

'Peace to his soul, if God's good pleasure be!'

THREE weeks had gone by since Dr. Cameron had written to Lord Paulyn, and Malcolm Forde still waited to hear the result of that application. He went on with his own particular work quietly enough in the mean while, did the heaviest part of the asthmatic curate's duty, read to all the bedridden cottagers within six miles of Hetheridge, went up to London every now and then to see his friends of the Gospel Society, and thus kept himself acquainted with all that was being done for the progress of that great work to which he had given his life, and so lived a not altogether empty or futile existence even during this period of self-abnegation. He had to attend a meeting in town one morning while still waiting for Lord Paulyn's letter, and finding his business finished at one o'clock, went straight to Eaton-place to call upon Miss Luttrell. He had heard from Dr. Cameron a day or two before, to the effect that there had been no answer from Lord Paulyn, but it was just possible Gertrude herself might have received a letter that very morning. The letter must come sooner or later, he thought, with some explanation of the delay which seemed so heartless.

The Eaton-place man-of-all-work—the man who had given Mr. Forde the ticket for the amateur theatricals at the Rancho—had rather a doubtful air when he asked to see Miss Luttrell. Mrs. Chevenix and Miss Luttrell were at home, he said, but he hardly thought they would see anybody.

'Miss Luttrell will not refuse to see me,' said Mr. Forde, giving the man his card.

'O, it's not that—I know you, sir, only I'm afraid there's something wrong. But I'll take your name in.'

He carried the card into the dining-room, and reappeared immediately to usher Mr. Forde in after it.

Mrs. Chevenix and her eldest niece were at luncheon, that is to say, the usual array of edibles— the snug little hot-water dish of cutlets, the imported pie in a crockery crust, the crisp passover biscuits, Stilton cheese, dry sherry, silver chocolate pot, and other vanities—had been duly set forth for Mrs. Chevenix's delectation, but that lady sat gazing absently at these preparations, with consternation written upon her countenance. Gertrude, who also sat idle at the other end of the table, was in the act of shedding tears.

'What is the matter?' Mr. Forde asked, with an alarmed tone. Had there been ill news from Hetheridge in his absence? His heart sank at the thought. But surely that could not be. He had inquired of the woman at the lodge that very morning, and had heard a good account of the patient. He had made this lodge-keeper his friend, bought her fidelity at a handsome price, at the very beginning of things, and so had been able to obtain tidings every day.

The two ladies sighed dolefully, but said nothing. There was an open letter lying beside Gertrude's plate, a letter edged with black. The letter from Lord Paulyn, he thought. That nobleman must be still in mourning for his mother.

'Have you heard from Rome?' he asked Gertrude; 'and does he forbid you seeing your sister? Can he be cruel enough, wicked enough to do that?'

'We have had no letter from Lord Paulyn, and I must beg you not to speak in that impetuous way about my poor nephew-in-law,' said Mrs. Chevenix. 'Lord Paulyn is in heaven.'

Malcolm Forde looked at her wonderingly; the phrase seemed almost meaningless at first.

'Yes, it's very dreadful,' said Gertrude, 'but it's only too true. I'm sure it seems like a dream. He was not a kind brother-in-law to me, and I had very little advantage from such a splendid connection, except, perhaps, being more looked up to and deferred to in Hawleigh society. The same people that asked us to spend the evening before Elizabeth's marriage asked us to dinner afterwards. Beyond that I had nothing to thank Lord Paulyn for. But still it seems so dreadful to be snatched away like that, and only thirty-four; and I fear that after the sadly worldly life he led here he'll find the change to a better world disappointing.'

'What do you mean?' asked Mr. Forde. 'Is Lord Paulyn dead?'

'Yes,' sighed Gertrude; 'the letter came this morning from his lawyer. He died at Rome last Thursday, after only a week's illness. He had been hunting in the Campagna, his lawyer says, and caught cold, but refused to stay in-doors and nurse himself, as his valet wanted him to do, and the next morning he woke in a high fever; and the landlord of the hotel sent for a doctor, an Italian, who bled him every other day to keep down the fever. But he grew rapidly worse, and died on Thursday morning, just as his servant began to get frightened and was going to call in an English doctor. The lawyer is very angry, and says he must have been murdered by that Italian doctor. It seems very dreadful.'

'It will be in the *Morning Post* to-morrow,' said Mrs. Chevenix solemnly. 'I shouldn't be surprised if they gave him half a column edged with black, like a prime minister. I suppose it would be a mockery to offer you luncheon, Mr. Forde,' she went on in a dreary voice; 'those cutlets *à la soubise* are sure to be good.' You won't? Then we may as well go up to the drawing-room. Give me a glass of sherry, Gertrude. I haven't touched a morsel of anything since breakfast.'

So they went up-stairs to the drawing-room—that room whose veriest trifles, the fernery, the celadon china, the lobsters and other sea-vermin in modern majolica ware, reminded Malcolm Forde of that bitter day when he had tried to cast Elizabeth Luttrell out of his heart as entirely as he banished her from his life.

'It seems like a dream,' said Gertrude, wiping away a tributary tear, and appeared to think that in this novel remark she had expressed all that could possibly be said about Lord Paulyn's untimely death.

'We shall all have to go into mourning,' she went on presently. 'So near Ashcombe, of course it would be impossible to avoid it, and I don't suppose he has left us anything for mourning; dying so suddenly, he wouldn't be likely to think of it. And the summer coming on too, with our dusty roads—positively ruinous for mourning.'

'He is to be brought home to Ashcombe,' said Mrs. Chevenix; 'and poor Elizabeth not able to be at the funeral. So sad! And her absence so likely to be noticed in the papers!'

They babbled on about funerals and mourning, and will or no will, while Malcolm Forde sat silent, really like one whose brain is entangled in the mazes of some wild dream. Dead!—the last, remotest possibility he could have dreamed of—dead! And Elizabeth set free, free for him to watch over, for him to cherish, for him to win slowly back to reason and to love!

He thought of her that night at Dunallen, that bitter night, in which temptation assailed him in the strongest form that ever the tempter wore for erring man's destruction, when she had stretched out her arms to him and pleaded 'Keep me with you, Malcolm, keep me with you!' and he had longed with a wild longing to clasp her to his breast, and carry her away to some secure haven of secrecy and loneliness, and defy the world and heaven and hell for her sake.

Brief but sharp had been the struggle; few the tears he had shed; but the tears a strong man sheds in such a moment are tears of blood. And behold, now she was free! He might say to her, 'Dearest, I will keep you and guard you for ever; and even if the lost light never comes back again—if those sweet eyes must see me for ever dimly through a cloud of troubled thoughts—I may still be your guardian, your companion, your brother, your friend.'

But she would recover—he had Dr. Cameron's assurance of that. She would recover. God would give her back to life and reason, and to him. How strange and new seemed that wondrous prospect of happiness! like a sudden break in a leaden storm-cloud flooding all the world with sunshine; like an opening in a wood revealing a fair summer landscape new to the gaze of the traveller, fairer than all that he had ever seen upon earth, almost as lovely as his dreams of heaven.

He sat speechless in this wonderful crisis of his life, not daring to thank God for this blessing, since it came to him by so dread a means, by the sudden cutting off of a man who had never injured him, and for whose untimely death he should have felt some natural Christianlike regret.

But he could not bring himself to consider his

dead rival, he could only think of his own new future —a future which would give back to him all he had surrendered—a future which would recompense him a thousandfold, even in this lower life, for every sacrifice of inclination, for every renunciation of self-interest, that he had made. It was not his theory that a man's works should be rewarded in this life; but earthly things are apt to be sweet even to a Christian, and to Malcolm Forde to-day it seemed that to win back the woman he had loved, to begin again from that unforgotten starting-point when he had held her in his arms under the March moonlight, the star-like eyes looking up at him full of unspeakable love, to recommence existence thus was to be young again, young in a world as new as Eden was to Adam when he woke in the dewy morning and beheld his helpmeet.

And Tongataboo, and the infantine souls who had wanted to worship him as their god, the dusky chiefs who made war upon each other and roasted each other alive upon occasion, only for the want of knowing better, and who were prompt to confess that the God of the Christians, not exacting human sacrifice or self-mutilation, must needs be 'a good fellow;' what of these and all those other heathen in the unexplored corners of the earth, to which he was to have carried the cross of Christ? Was he ready to renounce these at a breath, for the sake of his earthly love? No, a thousand times no! Love and duty should go hand-in-hand. His wife should go with him—should help him in his sacred work. He would know how to leave her in some secure shelter when the path he trod was perilous—he would expose her to no danger—but she might be near him always, and sometimes with him, and might help him in his labours, might serve the great cause even by her beauty and brightness—as birds and flowers, lovely useless things as we may deem them, swell the universal hymn wherewith God's creatures praise their Creator.

All these thoughts were in his mind, vistas of happiness to come, stretching in dazzling vision far away into the distant future, while he sat silent like a man spellbound, hearing and yet not hearing the voice of Mrs. Chevenix as she held forth at length upon the difference between real property and personal property in relation to a widow's thirds, and the supreme folly, the almost idiotcy—sad token of future derangement—which Elizabeth had shown in objecting to a marriage settlement.

'" Heir-presumptive,"' said Mrs. Chevenix, referring to Burke, whose crimson-bound volume lay open close at hand, '" Captain Paulyn, R.N.; born

January 1828; married, October 1849, Sarah Jane, third daughter of John Henry Towser, Esq., of West Hackney, Middlesex." Imagine a twopenny-halfpenny naval man inheriting that vast wealth, and perhaps Elizabeth left almost a pauper! If that sweet child had only lived! But there has seemed a fate against that poor girl from the first. What will be her feelings when she recovers her senses, poor child, and is told she is only a dowager! Even the diamonds, I suppose, will have to go to Sarah Jane, third daughter of John Henry Towser' (with ineffable disgust).

'As her nearest relation you will now have the right to see your sister without any one's permission,' said Mr. Forde to Gertrude, slowly awakening from that long dream. 'She has ceased to belong to any one—but you. Will you come up to Hetheridge to-morrow morning, Gertrude?' He had called her by her Christian name throughout this time of trouble, and to-day it seemed as if she were already his sister. He was eager to think and act for her, to do everything that might hasten the hour of Elizabeth's release.

'I will come if you like, only—there's the mourning; we can't be too quick about that. They may ask us to the funeral.'

'*They!* Who? Your brother-in-law had no near relations. There will only be lawyers and the new Viscount interested in this business. Let the dead bury their dead. You have your sister to think of. Could you not send for Blanche? Your sister expressed a desire to see Blanche. I have been thinking that I might find you a furnished house at Hetheridge; there is a pretty little cottage on the outskirts of the village, which I am told is usually let to strangers in summer. If I could get that for you now, you would be close at hand, and could see your sister daily. I have had a good deal of friendly talk with Dr. Cameron, and I am sure that he will do all in his power to hasten her recovery. May I try to secure the cottage for you?'

Gertrude looked at him curiously; she was very pale, and the eyes, which had once been handsome eyes, before time and disappointment had dimmed their lustre, had brightened with an unusual light— not a pleasant light.

'You think of no one but Elizabeth,' she said, her voice trembling a little. 'It is hardly respectful to the dead.'

'I think of the living whom I know more than of the dead whom I only saw for an hour or so once in my life; that is hardly strange. If you are indifferent to your sister's welfare at such a time as this, I will not trouble you about her. I can write to Blanche; she will come, I daresay, if I ask her.'

Blanche would come, yes, at the first bidding. Had she not been pestering her elder sister with piteous letters, entreating to be allowed to come to London and see her darling Lizzie, whose madness she would never believe in. It was all a plot of those horrid Paulyns. Gertrude knew very well that Blanche would come.

'You can take the cottage,' she said, 'if it is not very expensive. Please remember that we are poor. You won't mind my going away, will you, aunt, to be near Elizabeth?'

'My dear Gertrude, how can you ask such a question?' exclaimed Mrs. Chevenix expansively. 'As if I should for a moment allow any selfish desire of mine to stand between you and poor Elizabeth.'

She said this with real feeling; for Gertrude was not a vivacious companion, and her society had for some time been oppressive to Mrs. Chevenix.

It is no small trial for an elderly lady with a highly-cultivated selfishness to have to share her dainty little luncheons and careful little dinners, her decanter of Manzanilla, and her cup of choicest

Mocha, with a person who is neither profitable nor entertaining.

'Mr. Foljambe the lawyer, a person in Gray's-inn, promises to call to-morrow,' said Mrs. Chevenix presently. 'I suppose we shall hear all the sad particulars from him, and about the will, if there is a will.'

In the question of the will Mr. Forde felt small interest. Was he not rich enough for both, rich enough to go back to those sunny isles in the Southern Sea with his sweet young wife to bear him company; rich enough to build her a pleasant home in that land where before very long, if he so chose, he might write himself down Bishop? All his desires were bounded by the hope of her speedy recovery and release. He could go to Dr. Cameron now with a bolder front; could tell the kindly physician that brief and common story which the doctor had perhaps guessed at ere now; could venture to say to him, 'I have watched over and cared for her not only because I was her father's friend, and remember her in her bright youth, but because I have loved her as well as ever a woman was loved upon this earth.'

CHAPTER XVII.

> 'The widest land
> Doom takes to part us, leaves thy heart in mine
> With pulses that beat double. What I do
> And what I dream include thee, as the wine
> Must taste of its own grapes. And when I sue
> God for myself, He hears that name of thine,
> And sees within my eyes the tears of two.'

THE cottage was hired; a rustic little box of a place containing four rooms and a kitchen, with a lean-to roof; a habitation just redeemed from absolute commonness by a prettily-arranged garden, a green porch, and one bow window; but Gertrude, who came to Hetheridge with her worldly goods in a cab, declared the place charming, worthy of Mr. Forde's excellent taste. This was before noon upon the day after Malcolm heard of Lord Paulyn's death. He had lost no time, but had taken the cottage, engaged the woman who kept it to act as servant, seen Dr. Cameron, who had that morning received a letter from Mr. Foljambe the lawyer, and was inexpressibly shocked at the event which it announced, and had wrung from him a somewhat reluctant consent to the sisters seeing each other on the following day.

'There is a marked improvement; yes, I may venture to say a decided improvement; but Lady Paulyn is hardly as well as I could wish. The mind still wanders; nor is the physical health all I could desire. But that doubtless will be benefited by milder weather.'

'And freedom,' said Malcolm Forde eagerly. 'Elizabeth's soul is too wild a bird not to languish in a cage. Give her back to the scenes of her youth and the free air of heaven, and I will be responsible for the completion of her cure. You will not tell her of her husband's death yet a while, I suppose?'

'I think not. The shock might be too great in her present weak condition.'

Three o'clock in the afternoon was the hour Dr. Cameron appointed for the interview, and at half-past two Mr. Forde called at the cottage. He had promised to take Gertrude to the park gate, and to meet her in the Hetheridge road on her return, so that he might have early tidings of the interview.

It was a balmy afternoon in early spring, the leafless elms faintly stirred by one of those mild west winds which March sometimes steals from his younger brother April, an afternoon of sunshine and promise, which cheats the too hopeful soul with the fond delusion that summer was not very far off, that equinoctial gales are done with, and the hawthorn blossom ready to burst through the russet brown of the hedgerows. Hetheridge is a spot beautiful even in winter, essentially beautiful in spring, when the undulating pastures that slope away from the crest of the hill down to the very edge of the distant city are clothed in their freshest verdure, and dotted with wild purple crocuses, which flourish in profusion on some of the Hetheridge pastures. Hetheridge has as yet escaped the builder; half-a-dozen country houses, for the most part of the William-and-Mary period, are scattered along the rural-looking road, a few more clustered near the green. Shops there are none; only a village inn, with sweet-smelling white-curtained bed-chambers and humble sanded parlours, and a row of cottages, an avenue of ancient elms, and the village church to close the vista. At the church gates the road makes a sudden wind, and descends the hill gently, still keeping high above the distant city and the broad valley between, to the gates of Hetheridge Park.

'This bright afternoon seems a good omen,' said Malcolm Forde, as he and Gertrude came near this gate.

'O, dear Mr. Forde, surely *you* are not superstitious!' exclaimed Gertrude with a shocked air.

'Superstitious, no; but one is cheered by the sunshine. I am glad the sun will shine on your first meeting with your sister. Think of her, Gertrude, a prisoner on this lovely day!'

'But she is not a prisoner in the slightest degree. Don't you remember Dr. Cameron told us she was to have carriage airings?'

'Yes, to be driven out with other patients, I suppose, for a stiff little drive. I don't think Elizabeth would mistake that for liberty. This is the gate. I will leave you to find your own way to the house. I have no permission to cross the boundary. You will find me here when you come back.'

He waited a long hour, his imagination following Gertrude into that old red-brick mansion, his fancy seeing the face he loved almost as vividly as he had seen it with his bodily eyes that night at Dunallen. What would be the report? Would she strike Gertrude strangely, as a changed creature, not the sister she had known a year or two ago, but a being divided from her by a great gulf, distant, unapproachable, strange as the shadowy semblance of the very dead? It was an hour of unspeakable anxiety. All his future life seemed now to hang upon what Gertrude should tell him when she came out of that gate. At first he had walked backwards and forwards, for a distance of about a quarter of a mile, by the park fence. Later he could not do this, so eagerly did he expect Gertrude's return, but stood on the opposite side of the road, with his back against a stile, watching the gate.

She came out at last, walking slowly, with her veil down. His watch told him that she had been just a few minutes more than an hour, his heart would have made him believe he had waited half a day. She did not see him, and was walking towards the village, when he crossed the road and placed himself by her side.

'Well,' he cried eagerly, 'tell me everything, for God's sake! Did she know you? Was she pleased to see you? Did she talk reasonably, like her old self?'

Gertrude did not answer immediately. He repeated his question. 'For God's sake, tell me!'

'Yes,' she said, not looking up, 'she knew me, and seemed rather pleased, and talked of our old life at Hawleigh, and poor papa, and was very reasonable. I don't think there is much the matter with her mind.'

'Thank God, thank God! I knew He would be

good to us! I knew He would listen to our prayers! And she is better, nearly well! God bless that good Dr. Cameron! I was inclined to hate him at first, and to think that he meant to lock her up and hide her from us all the days of her life. But he only did what was right, and he has cured her. Gertrude, why do you keep your veil down like that, and your head bent so that I can't see your face? There is nothing to be unhappy about now that she is so much better. If she knew you and talked to you reasonably of the past, she must be very much better. You should be as glad as I am, as grateful for God's mercy to us.'

He took hold of her arm, trying to look into her face, but she turned away from him and burst into a passion of weeping.

'She is dying!' she said at last; 'I saw death in her face. She is dying; and I have helped to kill her!'

'Dying! Elizabeth dying!' He uttered the words mechanically, like a man half stunned by a terrible blow.

'She is dying!' Gertrude repeated with passionate persistence. 'Dr. Cameron may talk of her being only a little weak, and getting well again when the mild weather comes, but she will never live to see the summer. Those hollow cheeks, those bright, bright eyes, they pierced me to the heart. That was how mamma looked, just like that, a few months before she died. Just like Elizabeth, to-day. That little worrying cough, those hot dry hands—all, all the dreadful signs I know so well. O, Mr. Forde, for God's sake don't look at me like that, with that dreadful look in your face! You make me hate myself worse than ever, and I have hated myself bitterly enough ever since—'

'Ever since what?' he asked, with a sudden searching look in his eyes, his face white as the face of death. Had he not just received his death-blow, or the more cruel death-blow of all his sweet newborn hopes, his new life? 'Ever since what?' he repeated sternly.

She cowered and shrank before him, looking at the ground, and trembling like some hunted animal. 'Since I tried to part you and Elizabeth,' she said. 'I suppose it was very wicked, though I wrote only the truth. But everything has gone wrong with us since then. It seemed as if I had let loose a legion of troubles.'

'You tried to part us—you wrote only the truth! What! Then the anonymous letter that sowed the seeds of my besotted jealousy was your writing?'

'It was the truth, word for word as I heard it from Frederick Melvin.'

'And you wrote an anonymous letter—the meanest, vilest form which malice ever chooses for its cowardly assault—to part your sister and her lover! May I ask, Miss Luttrell, what I had done to deserve this from you?'

'That I will never tell you,' she said, looking up at him for the first time doggedly.

'I will not trouble you for your reasons. You did what you could to poison my life, and perhaps your sister's. And now you tell me she is dying. But she shall not die,' he cried passionately, 'if prayer and love can save her. I will wrestle for my darling, as Jacob wrestled with the angel. I will supplicate day and night; I will give her the best service of my heart and brain. If science and care and limitless love can save her, she shall be saved. But I think you had better go back to Devonshire, Miss Luttrell, and let me have your sister Blanche for my ally. It was not your letter that parted us, however. I was not quite weak enough to be frightened by any anonymous slander. It was my own hot-headed folly, or your sister's fatal pride, that severed us. Only I should hardly like to see you about her after what you have told me. There

would be something too much of Judas in the business.'

'O, Mr. Forde, how hard you are towards me! And I acted for the best,' said Gertrude, whimpering. 'I thought that I was only doing my duty towards you. I felt so sure that you and Elizabeth were unsuited to each other, that she could never make you happy—'

'Pray who taught you to take the measure of my capacity for happiness?' cried Mr. Forde with sudden passion. 'Your sister was the only woman who ever made me happy—' he checked himself, remembering that this was treason against that gentler soul he had loved and lost—'the only woman who ever made me forget everything in this world except herself. The only woman who could have kept me a bond slave at her feet, who could have put a distaff in my hand, and made me false to every purpose of my life. But that is all past now, and if God gives her back to me I will serve Him as truly as I love her.'

'Say that you forgive me, dear Mr. Forde,' pleaded Gertrude in a feeble piteous voice. 'You can't despise me more than I despise myself, and yet I acted with the belief that I was only doing my duty. It seemed right for you to know. I used to think it over in church even, and it seemed only right you should know. Do say that you forgive me!'

'Say that I forgive you!' cried Mr. Forde bitterly. 'What is the good of my forgiveness? Can it undo the great wrong you did if that letter parted us, if it turned the scale by so much as a feather's weight? I forgive you freely enough. I despise you too much to be angry.'

'O, that is very cruel!'

'Do you expect to gather grapes from the thorns you planted? Be content if the thorn has not stung you to death.'

'But you'll let me stay, won't you, Mr. Forde, and see my poor sister as often as Dr. Cameron will allow me? Remember, I was not obliged to confess this to you. I might have kept my secret for ever. You would never have suspected me.'

'Hardly. I knew it was a woman's work, but I could not think it was a sister's.'

'I told you of my own free will, blackened myself in your eyes, and if you are so hard upon me, where can I expect compassion? Let me stay, and do what I can to be a comfort to Elizabeth.'

'How can I be sure that you are sincere—that you really wish her well? You may be planning another anonymous letter. You may consider it your duty to come between us again.'

'What, with my sister on the brink of the grave?' cried Gertrude, bursting into tears — tears which seemed the outpouring of a genuine grief.

'So be it then. You shall stay, and I will try to forget you ever did that mean and wicked act.'

'You forgive me?'

'As I hope God has already forgiven you.'

CHAPTER XVIII.

'Now three years since
This had not seemed so good an end for me;
But in some wise all things wear round betimes
And wind up well.'

ELIZABETH has been nearly five months a widow. It is the end of July. She is at Penarthur, a little Cornish town by the sea, at the extreme western point of the land, a sheltered nook where the climate is almost as mild as the south of France; where myrtles climb over all the cottages, and roses blossom among the very chimney-pots; where the sea has the hues of a fine opal or a peacock's breast, for ever changing from blue to green. Penarthur is a combination of market-town and a fashionable watering-place; the town, with its narrow High-street, and bank, and post-office, and market, and busy-looking commercial inn, lying a little inland, the fashionable district consisting of a row of white-walled houses and one huge many-balconied hotel, six stories high, facing the Atlantic Ocean.

Among the white houses, there is one a little better than the rest standing alone in a small garden,. a garden full of roses and carnations, mignonette and sweet-peas, and here they have brought Elizabeth. They are all with her—Gertrude, Diana, and Blanche; Anne, the old vicarage nurse, who has left her comfortable retirement at Hawleigh to wait upon her darling; and Malcolm Forde, who lodges in a cottage near at hand, but who spends all his days with Elizabeth. With Elizabeth, for whom alone he seems to live in these bitter-sweet hours of close companionship; with Elizabeth, who is never to be his wife. God has restored her reason; but across the path that might have been so fair and free for these two to tread together there has crept the darkness of a shadow which forebodes the end of earthly hope.

He has her all to himself in these soft summer days, in this quiet haven by the sea, no touch of pride, no thought of conflicting duty to divide them; but he knows full surely that he will have her only for a little while; that the sweet eyes which look at him with love unspeakable are slowly, slowly fading; that the oval cheek, whose wasting line the drooping hair disguises, is growing more hollow day by day; that nothing love or science can do, and he has well-nigh exhausted the resources of both in her service, can delay their parting. Not upon this earth is he to reap the harvest of his labours; not in earthly happiness is he to find the fruition of his faith. The darkest hour of his life lies before him, and he knows it, sees the bolt ready to descend, and has to smile and be cheerful, and beguile his dear one with an aspect of unchanging serenity, lest by any betrayal of his grief he should shorten the brief span in which they may yet be together.

Physicians, the greatest in the land, have done their uttermost. She had lived too fast. That short reign of splendour in Park-lane, perpetual excitement, unceasing fatigue, unflagging high spirits or the appearance of high spirits, the wild grief that had followed her baby's death, the vain regrets that had racked her soul even in the midst of her brilliant career, the excitement and fever of an existence which was meant to be all pleasure—these were among the causes of her decline. There had been a complete exhaustion of vitality, though the amount of vitality had been exceptional; the ruin of a superb constitution, worn out untimely by sheer ill-usage.

'Men drink themselves to death very often,' said

one of the doctors to Malcolm Forde; 'and women just as often wear themselves to death. This lovely young woman has worn out a constitution which ought to have lasted till she was eighty. Very sad; a complete decline of vital force. The cough we might get over, patch up the lungs, or make the heart do their work; but the whole organisation is worn out.'

Mr. Forde had questioned them as to the possible advantages of change of climate. He was ready to carry her to the other end of the world, if Hope beckoned him.

'If she should live till October, you might take her to Madeira,' said his counsellor, 'though this climate is almost as good. The voyage might be beneficial, or might not. With so delicate an organisation to deal with, one can hardly tell.'

That disease, which is of all maladies the most delusive, allowed Elizabeth many hours of ease and even hopefulness. She did not see the fatal shadow that walked by her side. Never had the world seemed so fair to her or life so sweet. The only creature she had ever deeply loved was restored to her; a happy future waited for her. Her intervals of bodily suffering she regarded as an ordeal through which she must pass patiently, always cheered by that bright vision of the days to come, when she was to be Malcolm's helpmeet and fellow worker. The pain and weariness were hard to bear sometimes, but she bore them heroically, as only a tiresome detail in the great business of getting well; and after a night of fever and sleeplessness, would greet Malcolm's morning visit with a smile full of hope and love.

She was very fond of talking to him of their future, the strange world she was to see, the curious child-like people whose little children she was to teach; funny coloured children, with eyes blacker than the sloes in the Devonshire lanes, and flashing white teeth; children who would touch her white raiment with inquisitive little paws, and think her a goddess, and wonder why she did not spread her wings and soar away to the blue sky. Her brain was singularly active; the apathy which had been a distinguishing mark of her mental disorder a few months ago, which had even continued for some time after she left Hetheridge Hall, had now given place to all the old vivacity. She was full of schemes and fancies about that bright future; planned every room in the one-story house, bungalow-shaped, which Malcolm was to build for her; was never tired of hearing him describe those sunny islands in the Southern Sea.

They had been talking of these things one sultry afternoon, in a favourite spot of Elizabeth's, a little curve of the shore where there was a smooth stretch of sand, sheltered by a screen of rocks. She could not walk so far, but was brought here in a bath-chair, and sometimes, when weakest, reclined here on a couch made of carriage-rugs and air pillows. This afternoon they were alone. The three sisters had gone off on a pilgrimage to Mordred Castle, and had left them to the delight of each other's company.

'How nice it is to be with you like this!' Elizabeth said softly, putting a wasted little hand into Malcolm's broad palm, a hand which seemed smaller to him every time he clasped it. 'I wish there were more castles for the others to see, only that sounds ungrateful when they are so good to me. Do you know, Malcolm, I lie awake at night often —the cough keeps me awake a good deal, but it would be all the same if I had no cough—I lie and wonder at our happiness, wonder to think that God has given me all I ever desired; even now, after I played fast and loose with my treasure, and seemed to lose it utterly. I hope I am not glad of poor Reginald's death; he was always very good to me, you know, in his way; and I was not at all good to him in my way; but I can't help being happy even now, before the blackness has worn off my first mourning. It seems dreadful for a woman in widow's weeds to be so happy and planning a new life; but it is only going backwards. O, Malcolm, why were you so hard upon me that day? Think how many years of happiness we have lost!'

He was sitting on the ground by the side of her heaped-up pillows, but with his back almost turned upon her bed, his eyes looking seaward, haggard and tearless.

'You might as well answer me, Malcolm. But I suppose you do think me very wicked; only remember it was you first spoke of our new life together.'

'My darling, can I do anything but love you to distraction?' he said in utter helplessness. The hour would come, alas too soon, in which he must tell her the bitter truth; that on earth there was no such future for those two as the future she dreamed of; that her pilgrimage must end untimely, leaving him to tread his darkened path alone, verily a stranger and a pilgrim, with no abiding city, with nothing but the promise of a home on the farther shore of Death's chill river.

Would he meet her in that distant lánd? Yes, with all his heart and mind he believed in such a meeting. That he should see her as he saw her to-day, yet more lovely; that he would enter upon a new life, reunited with all he had loved on earth, united by a more spiritual communion, held together in a heavenly bondage, as fellow subjects and servants of his Master. But even with this assurance it was hard to part; man's earthborn nature clung to the hope of earthly bliss—to keep her with him here, now for a few years. The chalice of eternal bliss was hardly sweet enough to set against the bitterness of this present loss.

He must tell her, and very soon. They had often talked together of serious things during these summer days by the sea—talked long and earnestly; and Elizabeth's mind, which had once been so careless of great subjects, had assumed a gentle gravity; a spirituality that filled her lover with thankfulness and joy. But pure as he knew her soul to be, almost childlike in her unquestioning faith, full of penitence for the manifold errors of her short life, he dared not leave her in ignorance of the swift-coming change; dared not let her slip out of life unawares like an infant that dies in its mother's arms.

Should he tell her now; here in this sweet sunny loneliness, by this untroubled sea, calm as that sea of glass before the great white throne? The hot passionate tears welled up to his eyes at the very thought. How should he shape the words that should break her happy dream?

'Malcolm, what makes you so quiet this afternoon?' she asked, lifting herself a little on her pillows, in the endeavour to see his face, which he still kept steadily towards the sea. 'Are you beginning to change your mind about me? Are you sorry you promised to take me abroad with you, to make me a kind of junior partner in your work? You used to talk of our future with such enthusiasm, and now it is only I who go babbling on; and you sit silent staring at the sea-gulls, till I am startled all at once by the sound of my own voice in the utter stillness. *Have* you changed your mind, Malcolm? Don't be afraid to tell me the truth; because I love you far too well to be a hindrance to you. Perhaps you have reflected, and have begun to think it would be troublesome to have a wife with you in your new mission.'

'My dearest,' he said, turning to her at last, and holding her in his arms, her tired head lying upon his shoulder, 'my dearest, I never cherished so sweet a hope as the hope of spending all my future life with you; but God seldom gives a man that very blessing he longs for above all other things. It may be that it is not well for a man to say, "Upon that one object I set all my earthly hope." Our life here is only a journey; we have no right to desire it should be a paradise; it is not an inn, but a hospital. Darling, God has been very good to us in uniting us like this, even for a little while.'

'For a little while!' she cried, with a frightened look. 'Then you *do* mean to leave me!'

'Never, dear love. I will never leave you.'

'Why do you frighten me, then, by talking like that? Why do you let me build upon our future, till I can almost see the tropical trees and flowers, and the very house we are to live in, and then say that we are only to be together for a little while?'

'If you were to be called away, Elizabeth, to a brighter world than that you dream of, leaving me to finish my pilgrimage alone? It has been too sweet a dream, dearest. I gave my life to labour, and not to such supreme happiness; and now, they tell me, I am not to take you with me yonder. I am to have no such sweet companionship; only the memory of your love, and bitter lifelong regret.'

At this he broke down utterly, and could speak

no further word; but still strove desperately to stifle his sobs, to hide his agony from those fond questioning eyes.

'You mean that I am going to die,' she said very slowly, in a curious wondering tone; 'the doctors have told you that. O Malcolm, I am so sorry for you; and for myself, too. We should have been so happy; for I think I am cured of all my old faults, and should have gone on growing better for your sake. And I meant to be very good, Malcolm —never to be tired of trying to do good—so that some day you might have been almost proud of me; might have looked back upon this time and said, "After all, I did not do an utterly foolish thing in letting her love me."'

'Might have been;' 'should have been.' The words smote him to the heart.

'O my love,' he cried, 'live, live for my sake! Defy your doctors, and get well for my sake! We will not accept their doom. They have been false prophets before now; prove them false again. Come back to life and health, for my sake!'

She gave a little feeble sigh, looking at him pityingly with the too-brilliant eyes.

'No,' she said, 'I am afraid they are right this time; I have wondered a good deal to find that getting well was such a painful business. I am afraid they are right, Malcolm; and you will begin your new mission alone. It is better, perhaps, for all intents and purposes, except just a little frivolous happiness, which you can do without. You will have your great work still; God's blessing, and the praise of good men. What have I been in your life?'

'All the world to me, darling; all my world of earthly hope. Elizabeth,' in a voice that trembled ever so little, 'I have told you this because I thought it my duty. It was not right that you alone should be ignorant of our fears; that if—if that last great change were at hand, you should be in the smallest measure unprepared to meet it. But I do not despair; no, darling, our God may have pity upon us even yet, may grant our human wishes, and give us a few short years to spend together.'

'Strangers and pilgrims,' she said in a thoughtful voice. 'Pilgrims who have no abiding city. I was very foolish to think so much of our new life in a new world. The world where we shall meet is older than the stars.'

CHAPTER XIX.

> 'But dead! All's done with: wait who may,
> Watch and wear and wonder who will.
> O, my whole life that ends to-day!
> O, my soul's sentence, sounding still;
> "The woman is dead, that was none of his;
> And the man, that was none of hers, may go!"'

No gloomy forebodings, no selfish repinings ever fell from the lips of Elizabeth after that sad day by the sea. A gentle thoughtfulness, a sweet serenity, lent a mournful charm to her manner, and spiritualised her beauty. She was only sorry for *him*, for that faithful lover from whose side relentless Death too soon must call her away. Her own regrets had been of the briefest. These few summer months spent wholly with Malcolm Forde, in so perfect and complete a union, held enough happiness for a common lifetime.

'It cannot matter very much if one spreads one's life over years, or squanders it in a summer,' she said with her old smile, 'so long as one lives. I don't suppose all the rest of Cleopatra's jewels ever gave her

half so much pleasure as that one pearl she melted in vinegar. And if I had been with you for twenty summers, Malcolm, could we ever have had a happier one than this?'

'We have been very happy, darling. And if God spares you we may have many another summer as sweet as this.'

'If! But you know that will not be. O Malcolm, don't try to deceive me with false hopes, for fear you should end by deceiving yourself. Let us make the best of our brief span, without a thought beyond the present, except such thoughts as you will teach me—my education for heaven.'

The time came—alas, how swiftly!—when it would have been too bitter a mockery to speak of earthly hope, when these two—living to themselves alone, as if unconscious of an external world—and those about them, knew that the end was very near. The shadow hovered ever at her side. At any moment, like a sudden cloud that drifts across the sunlight, Death's mystic veil might fall upon the face Malcolm Forde loved, and leave them side by side, yet worlds asunder.

She was very patient, enduring pain and weakness with a gentle heroism that touched all around her.

'It is not much to suffer pain,' she said one day, when Malcolm had praised her patience, 'lying here, in the air and sunshine, with my hand in yours, after —after what I suffered last winter, in silence and solitude, with cruel jailers who dragged me about with their rough hands, and with my mind full of confused thoughts of you, thinking you were near me, that in the next moment you would appear and rescue me, and yet with a half consciousness of *that* being only a dream, and you far away. It seems very little to bear, this labouring breath and this hacking cough, after that.'

All his life was given up to her service, reading to her, talking to her, watching her fitful slumbers; for as she grew weaker her nights became still more wakeful, and she dozed at intervals through the day. All his reading was from one inspired volume; he had offered to read other things, lest she should weary of those divine pages, but she refused.

'I was not always religiously disposed,' she said; 'but in my most degenerate days I always felt the sublimity of the Bible.'

At her special request he read her all the Epistles of St. Paul, lingering upon particular chapters; she, in her stronger moments, questioning him earnestly about the great apostle.

'Do you know why my mind dwells so much upon St. Paul?' she asked him one day.

'There are a hundred reasons for your admiration of one who was only second to his Divine Master.'

'Yes, I have always appreciated his greatness in thought and deed; only there was another reason for my admiration—his likeness to you.'

'Elizabeth!' with a warning look, an old look which she remembered in the Hawleigh days, when his worshippers had all confessed to being more or less afraid of him.

'Is it wrong to make such a comparison? After all, you know, St. Paul was a human being before he was a saint. His fearlessness, his untiring energy, his exultant spirit, so strong in direst extremity, so great in the hour of peril, all remind me of you—or of what you seemed to me at Hawleigh. And you will go on in the same road, Malcolm, when I am no longer a stumbling-block and a hindrance in your way. You will go on, rejoicing through good and evil, with the great end always before you, like that first apostle of the Gentiles, whose strong right arm broke down the walls of heathendom. And I—if there were any thought or feeling in the grave—should be so proud of having once been loved by you!'

'Malcolm, I have a good deal of money, have I not?' she asked him one day. 'Aunt Chevenix told me I was left very well off, although Lord Paulyn died without a will. I was to have a third of his personal property, or something like that.'

'Yes, dearest.'

'And does that come to very much?'

'About seventy thousand pounds.'

'Seventy thousand!' she repeated, opening her eyes very wide; 'and to think how poor papa used to grumble about writing a cheque for four or five pounds. I wish I could have had a little of my seventy thousand advanced to me then. Ought I not to make a will, Malcolm?'

'It seems to me hardly necessary. Your sisters are your natural heirs, and they are the only people who would inherit.'

'They would have all my money, then?'

'Among them—yes.'

She made no farther inquiries, and he was glad to change the drift of their talk; but when he came at his usual hour next morning, he met a little man in black, attended by an overgrown youth with a blue bag, on the doorstep, and on the point of departing.

'Congratulate me on my business-like habits,

Malcolm,' Elizabeth said, smiling at him from her sofa by the window; 'I have just made my will.'

'My dearest, why trouble yourself to do that when we had already settled that no will was necessary?' he said, seating himself in the chair beside her pillows, a chair which was kept sacred to his use, the sisters yielding him the right to be nearest to her always at this time.

'I had not settled anything of the kind. Seventy thousand would have been a great deal too much for my sisters; it would have turned their heads. I have left them thirty thousand in—what do you call those things?—Consols; a sure three hundred a year for each of them, the lawyer says; and I have left five thousand to Hilda Disney, whom I always detested, but who has next to nothing of her own, poor creature. And the rest I have left to you—for your mission, Malcolm.'

He bent down to kiss the pale forehead, but words were slow to come. 'Let this be as you wish, dearest,' he said at last; 'I need no such remembrance of you, but it will be my proudest labour to raise a fitting memorial of your love. In every one of those islands I have told you about—God granting me life to complete the task—there shall be an English church dedicated to St. Elizabeth. Your name shall sound sweet in the ears of my proselytes at the farther end of the world.'

The end came soon after this. A sultry twilight, faint stars far apart in a cloudless opal sky—the last splendour of the sunset fading slowly along the edge of the western sea-line.

She was lying in her favourite spot by the open window, her sisters grouped at one end of the sofa, Malcolm in his place at the other, his strong arm supporting her, his shoulder the pillow for her tired head.

'Malcolm, do you remember the day of our picnic at Lawborough Beeches? Centuries ago, it seems to me.'

'Have I ever forgotten any day or hour we spent together? Yes, dear, I remember perfectly.'

'And how we went down the Tabor in that big clumsy old boat, and you told me the story of your first love?'

'Yes, dear, I remember.'

'You could never have guessed what a wicked creature I was that day. But you did think me ill-tempered, didn't you?'

'I feared I had grieved or offended you.'

'It was not temper, or grief, or anything of the

kind; it was sheer wickedness—wicked jealousy of that good girl who died. I envied her, Malcolm—envied her the joy of dying in your arms.'

No answer, save a passionate kiss on the cold forehead.

'I did not think it would be my turn one day,' she went on slowly, looking up at him with those lovely eyes clouded by death's awful shadow,—'I did not think that these dear arms would hold me too in life's last hour; that the last earthly sight my fading eyes should see would be the eyes I love. No, Malcolm, no; not with that look of pain! I am quite happy.'

THE END.